For my father,
Adiel Moncrief Jordan,
who taught by example that
when a cross burns in a yard, you show up to help
that very night,
and that money is not meant to be spent all on
yourself,
and that the teachings of Jesus ought to make people
nervous.

Joy Jordan-Lake

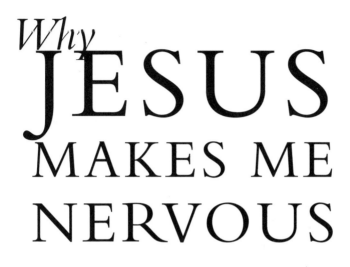

Why JESUS MAKES ME NERVOUS

Ten Alarming Words of Faith

PARACLETE PRESS

BREWSTER, MASSACHUSETTS

Why Jesus Makes Me Nervous: Ten Alarming Words of Faith

Copyright © 2007 Joy Jordan-Lake

ISBN 978-1-55725-520-4

Libaray of Congress Cataloging-in-Publication Data
Jordan-Lake, Joy. 1963–
    Why Jesus Makes Me Nervous–ten alarming words of faith / Joy
Jordan-Lake.
        p. cm.
ISBN 978-1-55725-520-4
1. Christian life.   I. Title.
BV4501.3.J67 2007
248.4--dc22   2007031276

10 9 8 7 6 5 4 3 2 1

Published by Paraclete Press
Brewster, Massachusetts
www.paracletepress.com

Printed in the United States of America

Contents

Foreword

Everything we know about God comes from what God has done in history. Unlike the ancient Greeks who made propositional statements about the essence of God, we are people who recognize that God is beyond anything that we can understand. What we do understand is what God does. We know that God loves us because of what God did in Christ on the cross. We know that God is at work in history because our eyes have seen the glory of His presence "in a hundred circling camps." We know that God is greater than all the other forces of the universe because we have read the stories of how God has confronted the principalities and powers of our age and defeated them. Unlike many of the other religions of the world, our faith is dependent on stories of what God has done in history, and it is a faith that continues to expand as we grapple with what God is doing in our own lives.

All of this is to say that what we believe is constructed from stories. The Gospels are stories and this is a good thing. That is because stories allow for the kinds of reflection that propositional statements can never provide. In the end, all theologies are simply commentaries on the stories.

Great things have happened to people as God has broken into their lives, and theologies are attempts to give rational explanations to others around us, trying to provide them with some understanding of what the stories have revealed to us. Of course, the stories are more profound than the theologies. As a case in point, the stories of the Crucifixion and the Resurrection have meanings that can never be fully explored or understood by human-made theologies. There is always more to them than those theologies can provide.

If heresies are presentations of truth that are only partial, then all theologies would be heresies, because the stories of Christ and the history of God in human affairs are too profound for any theology to holistically explore.

In a public forum, a friend of mine was asked, "Do you believe the story of the Creation, as told in the early chapters of Genesis, is literally true?"

My friend answered, "Oh! I believe that they are much *more* true than that!"

Ours is not a god who can be known objectively. God is not a thing! God is not an it! God is not some kind of creature that can be dissected and analyzed as high school sophomores dissect and analyze frogs. God is beyond all of that. Ours is a god who can only be known in encounters, and after those encounters there are attempts by the people who have experienced them to tell their stories to others. That's what the Bible is all about, and that's what Joy Jordan-Lake's book is all about. This is not to say that *Why Jesus Makes Me Nervous* is to be equated with the Bible, but it is to say that both are about real-life encounters.

Saint Francis of Assisi once said that people were sacramental. By that he meant that they are a means of grace, that the Christ who broke loose in history in Jesus—and gave Himself on the cross and was resurrected, and sent His Spirit to be in us—is waiting to be experienced in those people who confront us in our daily walks. Christ comes to us through them and we find new revelations of who He is as we enter into intimate relationships with those who cross our paths. We meet Him as some men on the shore of a lake once met Him. And we sense a presence, and if we are spiritually prepared, we are able to see God's face in the stranger. That's what Joy's book is about. Here we meet the Christ who broke loose in history. Here is the place of sacramentality.

Mother Teresa once said that whenever she looked into the eyes of a man dying of AIDS, she had an eerie awareness that Jesus was staring back at her. She was a woman who knew more about God than most of the theologians of our day. She didn't spend time reading theology or writing theology, but in her everyday encounters with those who were dying on the streets of Calcutta, she encountered Jesus. She always said that she received more from those that she served than she gave. She did not mean that there were "warm fuzzies" stirring around inside of her when she served others. She wasn't talking about the positive subjective reactions that occur when we live out altruism. Instead, she was referring to the revelations of God that were available to her whenever she looked into the faces of those whom she served. She was talking about what she learned of God through significant others who are sacramental revelations of that which transcends the categories of language and reason.

There is an old hymn that has, as an opening line, "Tell me the old, old story . . ." That hymn expresses what I am trying to say in this foreword. What follows in this book are stories that are new but capture the themes of the old, old story. They explore the meanings of the essential words that mark off what it means to be Christian. Like all good stories, they help us to feel the truth rather than just understand it. In the end, it is the felt truth that changes us and makes us into new creations. It is the truth that we *feel* in stories of the Bible that carries us beyond the categories of male and female when talking about God. Felt truth will enable us to see what eyes cannot see, hear what ears cannot hear, and touch what our hands cannot touch.

May the stories that follow not only introduce you to the feelings of the author, but equip you to have your own feelings derived from your own stories, in the hope that one day, when we all gather around the throne, we can share our stories with each other.

Tony Campolo, PhD
Professor Emeritus
Eastern University

Introduction

This book began in my understanding of how much I did not understand.

Throughout college and seminary and early graduate school, I took courses that offered profound, polysyllabic definitions for key words of the Christian faith: *resurrection*, for example. We scrawled spiral-bound pages of notes on how theologians define it. Who'd been martyred by whom for believing it. Which theories insisted on a physical rising from the dead and which suggested resurrection might be a revitalized belief in Jesus' followers. I took exams and wrote stuffy, poorly reasoned papers on the life of Jesus and his teachings. But it was later, outside the classroom, in the refining fires of real life, that I began experiencing—living into—the difficult and disconcerting and, frankly, appalling teachings of Jesus.

I've since learned that *resurrection* can be a matter of a moment's inner surrender but that living a real resurrection means passing through death.

I've learned that *community* offers support and warmth on the one hand, but also demands my helping shoulder heartaches that aren't directly my own.

That a*bundance* means living with a perpetual tug-of-war tension: living richly and living with riches can be opposite ends of the rope.

I've learned that *wisdom* begins in admitting how little our framed diplomas or professional titles reveal of who we truly are.

That *holiness* is not merely a matter of quick, easy grace, and that despite the clean-slate mercy he offers, Jesus ratchets up all the rules conducting our lives.

That *peace* may have little to do with a smooth-seas calm, and requires a ferocious hold on the truth.

That Jesus' definitions of the word *blessed* might seem sweet and unthreatening from a distance, but that the poor, the forgotten, the down and the out as Jesus sees them force me to rethink how I sort winners from losers, how I rethink my culture and my own life.

That true *worship* may depend more on my capacity for compassion than it does on a choir's hitting all the right chords.

That *forgiveness* sometimes means that destruction— rubble and dust and debris—must precede the beauty of rebuilding.

That *hope* draws its colossal power from its having once held hands with despair.

Jesus Makes Me Nervous approaches ten stained-glass words of faith—and then pries behind them to the unlovely buttressing on which they rest. This book attempts to explore just how uncomfortable Jesus can make things, telling stories of people who, because they buried, rather than used, what they'd been given, were bounced clear out of the club, of celebrations that begin with a wake, of a kind of abundance that grows in inverse proportion to the treasure-stockpiles of our lives.

Perhaps if we take the life and message of Jesus seriously—genuinely, even painfully—we'll see there are points along the path where we're intended to be made uneasy, seeing our guilt and brokenness. Maybe part of the power of the Good News comes from the bad: that new life blooms best out of the ashes. That the race that ultimately matters is a lifetime's distance-run toward holiness. Not the holiness that wears a prim, sour expression and white gloves, but the kind that takes risks and sports muddy boots, and takes a great deal of courage to follow.

Could it be that we are *meant* to be alarmed and disturbed and disrupted if we're to become people whose faith gains strength and force over the torrent of days into years?

Perhaps this is the outrageous challenge, and also the greatest of gifts: learning to live into these words, and grow a heart willing to be made nervous by Jesus.

1
Resurrection

He shows up advertising new life—this guy in sandals and a dust-crusted robe. A mangy crew tags along with him, some of them still smelling of salt water and spoiled fish. *New life*, he says, and in spite of yourself, you're falling for it: fresh starts, second chances, renewal, the dry, brittle bones of your past growing flesh and beginning again, with old hurts shed like a snake's skin on the grass. A little too good to be true, maybe, but awfully appealing, should it turn out to be true.

New life. Leaving the old stuff, the wreckage, the evidence of when you screwed up the last time and the forty-three times before that all strapped to barrels of concrete and dropped off the boat in the deep end of the ocean. Who wouldn't sign on for that?

So we hear the word *resurrection* in the days and hours before Easter, when the sweet breezes of spring buffet the rational parts of our brains into giddy submission. *Okay, well . . . maybe,* we're ready to say, as we watch the unlikely appearance of green from the brown, peeling bulbs we planted last fall. *Resurrection? Embarrassingly unscientific. Yet here's this warm soil that just last week was frozen to lifeless and now (who knew?) is willing to be worked once again. So what's a little more of the highly unlikely? Resurrection? Why the heck not? Bring it on.*

BUT.

But resurrection begins not with triumphantly toppled stones, empty tombs, and the masses agape in amazement, but before that. With death. With woundedness and mourning and betrayal, things done and undone, with understanding that dust and disaster and deceit are where we've landed.

Unless we're only looking at the final frame, resurrection is not pretty. To pretend otherwise, to make it, in John Updike's words, "less monstrous, / for our own convenience, our own sense of beauty," is to ignore its phenomenal power.

A minister friend of mine, Julie, has in her office a banner of truly remarkable tastelessness. It's enormous, with a garish orange sun whose red rays slide across bilious green hillocks: a toxic waste site with a Bible verse sunk beneath it.

It's hideous.

And I love it.

I love it partly because Julie insists it was made by a sweet, elderly former missionary to India. For all I know the little old saint will turn out to be the bouncer in heaven, ready to card me for heresy and un-Christlike aversion to flannel banners.

But I also love it for its hand-cut block letters that spell out "He Is Not Here. He Is Risen."

I've read those words when I hadn't eaten for days, when food had turned to dust in my mouth. I've read them and realized that perhaps I did not believe them—that I did not have that much hope anymore.

Risen. It's not a word you can play with safely, or the rough crowd it hangs out with: *resurrection.* Now there's a word you want to understand before you invite it inside. For one thing, it owes its entire existence to the prerequisite that something, or somebody, has died. To talk about resurrection, not just in Hallmark cards with rhyming verse, but on friendly terms, means you've already met up with brokenness and darkness, with the rubble of your bombed-out soul.

It turns out that the only people who can speak of resurrection with authenticity are the ones who've had a good whiff of the inside of a tomb. Resurrection is not a word you can tease and hold hands with for fun unless you're informed of the risks. Because to talk about resurrection like a personal friend is to talk first about your close acquaintance with death.

Resurrection, the way Jesus defines it, means you've already been visited by some unseemly company—like sin and those wages sin tries to keep charging. It's not, despite our hopes, the sin of the *Saturday Night Live* routine. Instead, it's flesh-and-blood real: sin showing up at your door demanding ongoing payment, throwing lamps and smashing the furniture, scaring off neighbors and family and friends by bull-horning the truth: that you're not *nearly* so good as you look, and here's why . . .

Raw and bloody: that's what Julie calls those places where you find you've shredded someone else's heart, or someone's ripped into yours, those seasons of the poor judgment of words or conduct: a crash you never saw coming—or chose not to. It's in these days and these places we're reminded we've sinned, messed up in high-definition proportions. And like David the Psalmist, the Beloved of God, David the Royal Screw Up, our sin can become an endless replay of regret.

We've been sinned against, too. Those times have left wounds splitting open and oozing again just when we thought they were healed.

At the southern tip of the Appalachians is a pretty little mountain that rings a pretty little city on a river. On the back side of this mountain is a road natives call the "W" road for its doubling back on itself as it ascends two thousand feet. If some thirty years ago you'd happened to be driving up this mountain in the dark and around on its precarious edge with the dawn of Easter Sunday just hours away, here's what you'd have stumbled onto: a small group of people huddled together in the cold. They are standing about clutching their hot cocoa and gnawing Krispy Kreme doughnuts in silence. Some of them are too cold to speak. Some of them, too sleepy. Some of them wonder *why in the world* they have come. Some of them have only come because of the doughnuts.

None of them look particularly extraordinary—with the possible exception of the little blonde girl with braids and buck teeth over there. She's quiet, you notice, and she's watching. You find yourself watching, too.

As they gather themselves into a circle and softly begin to sing, you notice this also: they're not remotely on key. But still, you can hear . . .

Were you there when they crucified my Lord? Were you there. . . . Sometimes it causes me to tremble. . . .

It's dark and now you're cold too and the fog mummies around you. You examine these people closely. You suspect it's a small place, this mountain, where everyone knows most everything about everyone. Even the little blonde girl with the buck teeth could tell you this much: that the lady over there with the round face and red mittens just last fall had her foot on the railing of the Market Street Bridge and was *so ready* to jump. And you might still see flickers of self-loathing and despair on her face.

The man in the lined hunting shirt: people whisper that he's the head of the local KKK chapter. It may be true. A few months ago, there was a cross burned, a family chased off the mountain.

It's *revolting*, you're thinking, that *he* would be here, here with you and the rest of these people waiting for Easter.

They're still singing, this group is, *Were you there.* . . .
Sometimes it causes me to tremble. . . .

There's also a man with a tie. Nobody told him you
don't have to dress up when it's still dark and still cold
and still only the hours *before* Easter. He's in the midst of
divorce. Everyone knows he hadn't really intended to end
his marriage. For years now, he'd thought somehow that
his money and *I'm sorry, honey* would be enough. And
then one day, it wasn't. He's quietly crying into his cocoa,
and he's squinting out into the dawn, not sure how it all
works, this thing they're all singing. Making no sound, his
shoulders shake a little. He's mouthing the words:

Were you there when he rose up from the grave. . . . *Sometimes
it causes me to tremble.* . . .

Then there's a woman in a soft, elegant coat. She's dark-
haired, gorgeous. Her voice soars pure and strong, perfect
pitch. Glancing at her, you might decide she's one of those
creatures whom life never hurts. Look closer. She'd dreamt
of singing at the Met one day. But she married, had three
kids. One of them is there right beside her. Watch her run
her hand over his hair, and over the thickness at the back
of his neck. He is smiling at her, his eyes nearly lost in the
swell of his cheeks. He has Down syndrome, you can see
for yourself. And you also see this: she loves him fiercely.

You watch as she sings with the others, *Were you there
when they laid him in the grave.* . . . *Sometimes it causes me to
tremble.* . . .

And there are more of these people, all gathered at the
edge of a mountain, huddled now shoulder to shoulder

against the cold, grasping their doughnuts and singing uncertainly, and peering out past the dogwoods to where, two thousand feet down, a woozy sun may soon be staggering up into the valley.

But right now it's only predawn darkness and doughnuts and raw, bloody pain—ancient rage and mangled hearts and a bunch of sleepy, shivering people trying to sing together on key. All of them privately wondering if they could even begin once more to believe in resurrection.

Sometimes, they sing, *it causes me to tremble. . . . Were you there. . . ?*

There in the fog before dawn, they feel strangely drawn to this idea of death. To death and to life—and to Jesus. That last one in some ways is the strangest of all.

In these days and hours before Easter, days of ashes and dark, we realize that we're sick and we're dying and we're dead, and that finally these can be the beginning of life.

There's a seventeenth-century poet I love, a one-time playboy turned Anglican priest: John Donne first excelled at seduction poems; later, he crafted lines full of a new, violent desire for intimacy and beginning again. "Batter my heart, three-personed God; for You / As yet but knock, breathe, shine, and seek to mend; / That I may rise and stand, o'erthrow me, and bend / Your force to break, blow, burn, and make me new."

These are the dark days. These are the hours when we can fall at the feet of the one who was lifted up for our sakes: Jesus raw and bloody rising up from the dead.

And if the violence of this process of new life is frightening for us, then that's as it should be. In the gospel accounts of the empty tomb, fear is the common element—the writers mention trembling and fleeing, tears and bewilderment, mixed in some cases with joy. But fear comes first. In Luke, it's only in their fright that the women remember the words Jesus spoke about his resurrection, not before.

When I worked with friends in New England to begin a clothes closet and food pantry for homeless families, we explained our worthy cause to various Boston-area department stores and asked for clothing racks they could spare. One Cambridge store manager grudgingly told us to stop by. Two fellows, one who owned an ancient but helpfully huge gray station wagon, went with me. They'd both grown up in Cambridge, and had been, by their own accounts, infamous ruffians in that neighborhood. But through a couple of unlikely encounters, including passing by a concert in a VFW hall from which lyrics, painfully authentic, pierced into the night, these two had both, against all odds, passed through death.

The store's salesperson met me at the loading dock and disinterestedly heard me express our undying thanks for the one little rack she donated. Then she caught sight of the two rough characters she remembered from school years. *Terror* took hold of her face.

Pete and Jay R. explained that they'd come to help load the donated rack, and how they'd come to this post-death season of life.

No, she said. *No way.*

They spoke of a sunrise that came, unlooked for.

She listened, her eyes shifting back toward the door where she could still make her escape.

But in her bewilderment and her fear, she loaded us with as many clothing racks as the old gray wagon could hold, and might have emptied the store had Pete's car been able to hold more.

As we drove away, waving, she was still pale and clutching the wall to steady herself.

Sometimes it causes me to tremble. . . .

My husband and I got word this week that an old friend of ours is in trouble. Our friend had a string of impressive degrees from a series of Ivy League schools, a postcard-perfect family and a fine, gentle, generous heart, one after God's own. But our friend's life now includes a meth addiction. Pornography. Hookers. Arrests. Abuse. Divorce. And restraining orders. A life all come undone.

Sometimes it causes me to tremble. . . . Were you there when they crucified my Lord . . . ?

Partly what's so terrifying about our friend's life is that it's mine too—any of ours. It's as my friend Kelly once said: "There's a snake that lies coiled around all our hearts, only we mostly don't know it's there." Maybe, I'd add, because we choose not to know.

This most assuredly describes me and maybe you, too. And it's the impossible that we're there on the mountain waiting for: that whatever we've shredded, made raw and bloody and way past repair, could maybe one day have life breathed into it again.

"Formation-by-resurrection" is how Eugene Peterson describes what we're to be about as people of faith. Indeed, it's in learning to see ourselves as created, or re-created, by the *before* and *after* distinctions, and telling those stories, giving life to those pictures, that we live into the Resurrection.

There is pain in this world, plenty of it—pain that is ancient and still newly ripped open. Tempers that come untethered. Dark, scary places we hope the people in our office can't see. Words we use as weapons; trust we can batter. There is apathy and alienation, disgust and deceit.

And there is Jesus.

Tombs emptied out.

The raw and bloody rising up from the dead. *Resurrection.*

Were you there when he rose up from the grave. . . . Sometimes it causes me to tremble. . . .

There are ends, but also beginnings.

I believe in all the cracks in my own plaster and the rotting it hides, all the moldering holes in my heart.

I believe fair-haired saints can become addicted to meth.

But I believe also in gluttonous worms who gorge themselves drunk on my garden's best leaves, bed themselves down on tree twigs, then wake up in spring with bold, bright-colored wings.

I believe sunrises and new days can happen for eaters of Krispy Kreme doughnuts and off-key singers of hymns and bigoted burners of crosses.

I believe in the gangrenous state of my own spirit, left to itself. And the slow, steady rehab brought on by mercy. In lives changed against all the odds.

In middle-aged women who don't jump off bridges but live instead to become much-loved grandmothers, and in old men who can weep over where they went wrong.

In a place where our last tears will be caught by God's hand, a time when "death, thou shalt die."

Death, it turns out, has to come first.

It's the one door into the blowout, the jazz band and swing-dancing and toasting, the party that's thrown when the dead live again, and come home.

Someday maybe I'll sneak into Julie's office and spray paint my own little additions to her remarkably tasteless banner:

HE IS NOT HERE.

And neither am I

HE IS RISEN.

Me too

For in the days and hours before resurrection, there are songs sung weakly and not at all well over the edge of small mountains; there are daffodils sprung out of just-frozen soil. Beauty rising up out of the ashes we make of our lives, the havoc we wreak. There is forgiveness and healing and hope.

There is Jesus.

And when we're up on the mountain and waiting for sunrise, if we catch ourselves in a tremble, maybe that means we're being formed. By death. And by resurrection.

2
Community

Is it harsh to suggest that they're simply not telling the truth—the whole truth—all those gilt greeting cards, those gentle souls who insist that sharing our burdens leaves us all lighter and brighter?

I don't mean they're *intending* to gloss things over into a lie, these people who are liable to launch into a rousing chorus of "Climb, Climb Up Sunshine Mountain" sung from metal folding chairs in basement *fellowship* halls. These sweet-spirited saints should be loved. But not trusted.

Real Christian community has little to do with Sunshine Mountain.

Real community is more like my friend Janet watching me sob into my rosemary bread at a Quizno's in Texas.

Janet and I had become friends when we'd moved to Texas at about the same time and discovered we shared a peculiar disorder: finding comfort in the heady aromas of equine sweet feed and leather and aging manure.

She'd invited me one August day on a trail ride through brittle sage and sun-stroked mesquite, and she'd shown herself to be the far better horsewoman. As we pulled the tack from our mounts, Janet told how she'd met her husband, Bob, working in the kitchen of a camp in the Rockies, the same camp where their daughter, Joanna, would work that next summer.

That day at Quizno's, in fact, we spoke of Janet's daughter. Joanna was a young beauty of still more beautiful spiritual depth. Authentic. Vivacious. A leader of her high school's Young Life Chapter. When she'd spoken of her journey of faith at a recent fund-raising event, she'd glowed. Flushed cheeks, bright eyes, a spill of long, yellow hair, and a laugh that kept fizzing up into her words.

But then here we were, these many months later, in Quizno's, nearby diners turning to stare as I blew my nose in a napkin.

Janet was speaking of Joanna.

The day after her eighteenth birthday, Joanna and two friends had driven the ninety miles south to Austin for lunch. They were celebrating their upcoming graduations from high school, her birthday, their recent prom, the gleam of their futures before them. They'd laughed 'til they hurt. They'd been girlfriends out together, young and carefree.

On the way home, they'd pulled off for soft drinks, and

in pulling back onto the access road, failed to yield to another driver. The two girls in the front seat, one of them Joanna, were killed.

The call had come to my house late that night, my husband out of town, my infant son cocooned in his crib, my older daughter asleep in my bed, my younger daughter still only a dream and a prayer. I lay awake all that night, stunned beyond all reaches of sleep, and stroked my own daughter's long hair. I tried to form prayers, but mostly let the hole blasted through my insides do the speaking to God. If I slept at all, it was as monks do between Divine Offices of the night, my words going forth in choked gutterals: *oh God, dear God, oh God, God, Jesus, dear God, oh God, God, GOD.* . . .

The next day I'd gone to Janet's house, where family and nearly the entirety of their old church in Ohio were beginning to gather. My '96 Taurus began wheezing just as I pulled onto their street, and actually cut off its own motor just outside their door. So I arrived to be of assistance with a platter of sandwiches, a potted plant, and a broken-down car.

Not being one of the innermost circle of friends, and never one to find the right words in a crisis, I mourned alongside the others, like me nearly silent, all of us washing dishes and replenishing platters and fielding phone calls. Then, whispering into a corner, I phoned AAA to come tow my car.

But tipped off by someone, Janet stopped me. "Bob's already out there looking at it."

"*What!*"

"He loves working on cars."

Her husband, Bob, was a dean at the university where we all worked. He wore suits to work and was known for innovations in public education. His daughter had just been killed the night before.

And he was working on my car.

"But he . . . I can't—!"

"Let him," she said.

I ran out to the car, its hood still steaming.

Bob was indeed bending over my engine, two men flanking him.

I opened my mouth to beg Bob to stop.

One of the men laid a hand on my arm. "Let him. You need to let him."

Back inside, Janet nodded. "At least for these moments, he can focus on something that isn't this. For these moments at least, it's a gift."

Four months later, my friend Janet sat square shouldered and without tears, but with grief in her eyes that suggested she was still hemorrhaging on the inside, telling me of her prayer life from deep down in the Valley of the Shadow, while I wept. For us, there was no mercy of a conked-out car engine to focus on and, for a moment at least, pretend that's why we were there.

Up to that point, it had been a nice day. The lecture on Walt Whitman had gone well, though I've never much cared for Whitman. Several students had lagged after class to talk—a good sign.

Having lunch with Janet had ruined all that. Just by her being honest and real, not pretending that things were happier, sweeter, more easy to bear than back in May, she'd drawn me into her valley of empty-armed darkness. Here she soldiered on, dressing and driving and breathing, just as if the world were still a blue-skies kind of place and not what she knew it to be. Praying and believing in hope, against all the evidence.

We were community that day at Quizno's. And it wasn't pretty.

I have no illusions that people outside Christian faith don't share grief and delight with their friends, that they aren't drawn into the same harbors of sorrow and celebration. Or that people who've at least commenced some kind of conversation with Jesus become automatically, *presto*, somehow superior at creating communities of the real and the free and the brave.

It's just that Christ, on the night he was betrayed, made it nonnegotiable, this community thing. For the crowd who shows up with Jesus, it's part of the deal, part of what you signed on for. *Community*. Sometimes fuzzy and pink and straight out of the hospital gift shop. Sometimes raw and mind-numbingly painful. It's learning to peel back the husks of I'M NICE AND IN NO NEED OF HELP on ourselves and the person beside us, and not passing out when we see what's inside.

In the 1980s, my husband worked with the Peace Corps in Paraguay, where he learned the native, pre-Spanish language, Guarani. I speak an impressive word total of two Guarani words: *nande* and *ore* (pronounced yan-day and ore-ay). Both mean "we" or "our," but the latter excludes the person you're speaking to, while the former, *nande*, includes that person. It's always struck me as a helpful communications fine point we should require in English. It would clear up so many awkward social situations if one could state from the beginning that *only ORE were invited, in other words, not you, and please don't press me for why.*

But the kind of community Jesus creates that last, rented-room night hanging out with the boys from the 'hood starts out with "I" and "you," and ends up, by the breaking of a body and the shedding of blood, creating a "we" that draws everyone—those who want to be drawn—in for the grim days ahead, a *nande* kind of "we." Whether you like it or not, you're included. If you're noshing the bread and downing the wine, you're along for the ride. For the good, bad, and ugly, you're part of the team.

It struck me a number of years ago when I was helping to serve communion in New England what a strange and radical practice it was.

Take the word we use for it: *communion*. Do we really mean that?

We're tough, self-reliant. We can do it all on our own. Communion, indeed. With God, maybe—but *only* God, and only as I conceive of God, and only while the music plays softly and the light streams through the hues of century-old stained glass.

You know how it goes. The movement is no longer connected in any meaningful way to the conscious mind.

But now and then the whole thing takes you by surprise, the words *This is my body, This is my blood* seep quietly into and fill the hole inside you'd forgotten was even there. It's only for that moment, only as you reach for the bread, the body given for you, and accept the cup, the blood shed for you, that you feel somehow linked with the divine, certain for that fleeting moment that you are looked upon with mercy and love. You are still marveling at the part about you—given for *you,* shed for *you*—when the person behind you steps up to your place to receive the words *This is my body, given for. . . .*

And it's not just that one person. There are two long lines of people staggering out of their pews, going through the motions whether they believe it or not just now. And over and over again the words *This is my body, given for. . . . This is my blood, shed for . . .* meet them as they come, building face upon face and life upon life until the words mean something more than just you.

Before you and behind you and to your side these others reach for the bread and drink from the cup, having lugged well-disguised fears, ravenous greeds, secret selves, dearest dreams. As they come and come and come, again and again and again, those words come too, as if they had not been whispered to the person before him or the person after her, but spoken as if they mean something very different and very much the same each time.

There's the one whose future looks murky. The present is polluted, mostly by his own decisions. He knows that, and treading water is no longer an option. *This is my body,* he hears. *And my blood, shed for you.*

There's another coming forward, who feels within her another life, carving out spacious new caverns for itself beneath her ribs. Sometimes she finds herself startled by a kind of joy that tumbles from somewhere deep within her.

She too hears, *This is my body. This is my blood, for you. For us. Nande.*

There are others, though, who let their eyes wander discreetly around the room, and feel oddly cramped and crowded—and alone. Tired of being alone. Tired of concocting ecstatic remarks about other people's engagement rings and mustering up little cooing sounds for other people's babies. So tired of being cramped and crowded and all alone.

This is my body. This is my blood.

Others come not allowing themselves to think out loud about the little pulses of doubt in the goodness or the justice of God that throb inside their heads. And some of them spend a good portion of their days punching on a difficult past, beating it back into its flimsy box where it does not stay for long. Still others coming now have watched sickness come stalking, watched mighty medical weapons crumple like cardboard swords and somehow still managed to hear *This is my body. This is my blood, shed for you . . . shed with you.*

Face after face and life upon life, and you discover that shared pain is not lessened pain. Quite the opposite. Her pain and his pain and their pain have all become your pain too. Somehow the pain becomes greater when it is passed around.

But so does the healing.

And the hope.

This is my body. This is my blood.

Christ speaks among us and something peculiar happens: You and I and they are all marking our seven-year anniversary without a date; we are all approaching ninety-five and widowed; we are all getting married in June. We are all facing cardiac surgery next week. We are all on public assistance, permanently unemployed; we all drive broken-down heaps.

Christian community, taken seriously, means suddenly you're shouldering the tragedies, the abandonment, the grief of the people around you, just as they're shouldering yours. Community means sharing each other's joy and hope and healing. In a thousand ways, taking Jesus seriously makes life harder, tougher, uglier.

And richer. Finer. Finally worth living.

The last time I saw my friend Janet before we both moved away from Texas, she was out walking in our neighborhood. She'd been in Colorado a great deal, and had buried Joanna's ashes there. I'd traveled all summer myself, so it was unusual for us to see more of each other than our frowzy front lawns.

I asked her how she was doing.

She told me the truth. Without tears. Or self-pity. It wasn't pretty. How could it be? How could you live a single day, or the shard of an hour, without missing your child's laugh, her way of cocking her head at a joke?

Yet there Janet stood, speaking of a drawn-and-quartering pain, matter-of-factly. And speaking of prayer.

Then she asked me how I was doing.

I took a deep breath.

Did I tell her the truth? Was it appallingly callous to ask a woman who'd lost her daughter sixteen months earlier to pray about the possible adoption of mine?

I looked at her face. What she'd given me was the truth, scarred and bruised and unadorned. She was standing there expecting the same kind of frankness from me.

"Well . . . it's been kind of a rough patch of road lately, my life. I mean . . . not like. . . ." I was already ashamed, sounding like my troubles were weighty compared to hers.

She looked me up and down. "I can see that," she said. Perhaps it was the circles under my eyes. Perhaps she could see I'd dropped weight.

Her eyes not leaving mine, she waited for more.

"We're . . . struggling with whether or not to go through with the adoption. It's pretty complex. But . . . it's . . . been a tough time."

She nodded. She didn't seem to need to know the

specifics of just what kind of rough patch of road it might
be. Or why. She just took in the fact that it was, from my
lips and from my eyes, and perhaps from my jeans hanging
loose from my hips. Just that it was.

She was watching me closely. "You felt God called you to
do this when you began this process?" she asked.

That one was easy. "Yes." And I could have added, "For
years—years even before the biological children."

"You still feel God has called you to do this?" she wanted
to know.

I feel, I wanted to cry, *as if we've had a child die.* But how
could I possibly understand that kind of heart-shredding
sorrow she knew? I did know, though, what a miscarriage
felt like, and pulling out of this adoption felt so much like
that, I sometimes fully expected some sort of bodily fluid to
break open inside me.

"Yes" was all I got out.

She nodded again. "Then I'll pray," she said, watching me
still. "For clarity. And for peace."

We hugged. Janet did not often hug. I knew this for the
offering it was.

She left for Colorado again, this time for a several-month
trip. Before she returned, I'd moved to Tennessee. It was the
last time I saw her. But I know she prayed.

Clarity did come.

And peace.

And then a gorgeous baby girl from Hunan who is
pure gift.

I know Janet prayed, the heart cries of a mother who

had to tell her own daughter good-bye, praying for the arrival of mine.

And I, who received a new baby daughter, continue praying for Janet. Frankly, praying makes many days less mindlessly happy. As it should be. Praying for Janet reminds me to pray for others buried up to their shoulders in sorrow. It also makes me more conscious of counting out the moments of joy, of little hands in my hand, more able to weigh the heavy treasure of love.

I know that she prayed. Just as I pray for her. Because we've sat down at the same table: *This is my body. This is my blood, shed for you. And for you.* Creating an *us*.

We are all staggering under the grief, hardly able to breathe, the loss of our child like lead weights upon us; we are all embracing a new family member.

We are sadder than when we first got here. But kinder, too.

Wiser. And more free with our tears.

We are many and we are one and we are happy and hurt and much, so much, in need of grace, of hearing

This is my body. This is my blood. Shed for you. And for you. Shed for us.

Nande.

Abundance

Nearly every time he speaks for any length of time, mostly to tell stories or to suggest to the disciples they've missed the point once again, Jesus finds a way to work in some thoughts on living abundantly. On how to get rich. On how to be blessed.

Only he'd never have made the best-seller list, given that his road to riches and security always begins with emptying out—of possessions, of self. In Jesus' vision of an idyllic lifestyle, there's not much glitz, glamour, or magazine cover potential. Instead of tips on turning the perfect real estate trick, or investing in venture capital, Jesus ignores the crowds to listen to the poor mother on public assistance. When he's approached by the earnest young Fortune 500 CEO, Jesus doesn't offer sound institutional sense with start-up ideas and good financial backing. Nor does Jesus pat the guy on the back for having penciled all the right boxes in the commandments checklist. Instead, Jesus bluntly—with a compassionate look in his eye—counsels the young man to cash in his stock and give the proceeds away. All proceeds. The big place at the beach *and* the penthouse in the city. The Italian sports cars *and* the yacht. Give your riches away if you want to live richly.

The wealthy young model citizen turns back, disheartened and thoroughly rattled.

And if we were in his designer shoes? So would we.

Or maybe I should speak for myself.

At the root of my spiritual problems is horse fencing—that is, coveting my neighbor's horse fencing. Not the silver Jaguar that pulled up beside me this morning at the light, nor the latest technological toy. Show me Armani suits and diamond pendants: I'm rarely rendered comatose with envy.

Horse fencing, on the other hand, four-board wooden affairs that stretch for miles over rolling pastures that frame in four-legged equine. Oh my. And the cupola-crowned barns that go alongside. The sweet scents of fine leather and fresh hay. These expose my true spiritual state.

For me, covetousness and unbridled greed are always only one stable away.

In *The Great Gatsby*, Daisy Buchanan is brought to worshipful tears by the sight of Gatsby's closet full of silk shirts. She buries her face in a handful of them. Me, I get weak in the knees over aging manure and brass nameplates on long lines of Dutch doors.

The story Jesus tells of the man who builds a bigger barn and then a bigger barn still has always made a great deal of sense to me. The man whom children's Bible storybooks make out to be a goofy buffoon as he believes his flourishing crops merit a finer structure is to me a kindred spirit. A barn the size of a small cathedral? Who *wouldn't* want that? Except the story as Jesus tells it ends badly, with the man keeling over in his own bedroom—his last view out the window, his fabulous barn.

Now, I live in a gorgeous community. If I drove you around in my boxy blue Kia, you would agree. The rolling hills, the lush landscaping, the magnificent marching forward of seasons, autumn leaves with war paint and glistening blown-glass branches in winter and weeping cherry trees on every corner in spring. Some of this is natural, a land carved by rivers and wind and the playful hand of God, who prefers these acres of Tennessee to all other parts of the earth and therefore spends more time here. But some of this beauty is created by landscaping companies hiring undocumented workers who toil away for, at best, minimum wage.

I live here amongst all this beauty, the natural and the expensively crafted. Worse, I love living here. My house shrinks weekly as the homes being erected around us continue to rise: the wine cellars accessed by elevators, the travertine tile, the marble and mahogany. Our house is dwarfed to downright ascetic alongside the Rhine Valley castles just a ball's toss away.

And yet. . . .

My husband is on one or two matters a scrinch closer to Jesus than I am. He insists that his dream home for our family of five is a square-footage that's snug and decidedly self-sacrificial. It's a goal I appreciate for its spiritual depth. Though when one child is practicing piano in one room and another is napping and a third is singing to himself as he colors and my husband is blasting Bob Dylan from the garage and I'm on the laptop hoping to hear myself think, I appreciate the structure of our house. At these times, I try to convince myself Jesus would find this a pleasant place to sit down for coffee and we would be able to actually hear one another over the dull roar.

I could be wrong about Jesus and coffee.

We have an agreement, my husband and I. I've offered to arrive in heaven with matching T-shirts for the two of us. The front of his shirt will read

The excess square footage was her fault.

Mine will say

And everything else was his.

But amidst the playful, I hear the prophetic always and everywhere in my ear.

I don't particularly want to pay attention to Jesus. Not on this issue.

But I desperately want that freedom that comes from slipping out of the grip of my own greed.

And on a good day, I am wanting to listen. Aware that my grasps at abundance leave me feeling cheap and overstuffed, more hungry and needy than ever.

On a good day, I desire depth and a compassionate heart more than I desire material things. But all days are not good.

On a good day, I'm wary of becoming what T.S. Eliot described as a "decent godless people / Their only monument the asphalt road / And a thousand lost golf balls."

Or a thousand empty shopping bags.

A thousand takeout food containers.

Not long ago, I complained to a friend Chuck, an Episcopal priest, that the house we owned in Texas still had not sold and the extra mortgage payments, with us now a thousand miles east, were painful. We were beginning to think, I told my friend, of simply giving the house away— *did St. Paul's church need a homeless shelter or another rectory? Maybe God would be willing to negotiate with me on the lost equity: a trim in the next several years' tithing percentage?* I was kidding. Mostly. Perhaps not entirely.

My friend answered by e-mail: *How can God negotiate with us when all we have, all we are, is God's? What can we bring to the table?* He quoted Miroslav Volf: that what we give to God's right hand is only what we've taken from God's left.

Turning from the computer, I slunk away through my house, through the stuff-abundance around me.

Some days, the material muchness around me rests heavily on my shoulders. Perhaps these are the good days. The days when I'm aware of God's abundance, not mine.

It helps me to think of all money as Monopoly tender. As if it's play money, only mine for the course of the game, and not necessarily to be used for buying Park Place, then annihilating other players for daring to set their metal dog on what is mine. *Very, VERY mine,* as my three-year-old likes to say.

What if this were not mine at all, only given to me like the flimsy one-sided yellows and pinks and lime greens of the game?

Years ago, for a seminary class assignment, I spent the night at a homeless shelter in Louisville, Kentucky. A young woman running from an abusive husband struck up a friendship with me. I volunteered little about who I was but offered my name. She assumed we were much in the same dire straits. We shared breakfast at the shelter, side by side, and both spoke of our dreams for the future. She asked if I had any money. I didn't. Not on me, at least.

So she offered to give me the only money she had in the world, the money she'd earned by selling her own blood the previous day. Giving it to me, a virtual stranger, because I was homeless and desperate like her, she assumed, and because she had it to give.

Her abundance. God's abundance. Offered to me. Me, well-fed, with a dozen safety nets to break my fall should I ever lose a job or miss a meal.

Yet here was her abundance. Fifteen dollars. All she had, offered to me.

There I stood, stunned. A graduate student, already a thousand times privileged for the luxury of education, being offered bounty from the heart and the pocket—the actual blood—of an abused homeless woman.

"God sees us," she told me. "God knows we need help. Here . . . let me help you with this." She tried to press a couple of bills in my hand—her only money in the world at that moment. She would trust me, she said, to pay her back as soon as I could.

I didn't take the money she offered.

But neither did I manage to find her after that day, and see how, from the world where I lived, I might help her.

In the years since then, I've often thought of this woman. I like to think she lives richly.

I suspect that, according to Jesus, she does.

Because she understood far better than I did about abundance, and whose hand it comes from.

God's. Taken from the left hand and offered back to the right.

4 Wisdom

When I began PhD studies
at a university just outside
Boston, it was whispered that I was from a tiny
town somewhere in that illiterate backwater, The South,
and that even now I worked part time for a Baptist—*oh
dear God, no, not a Baptist*—church. The evidence was clear:
the Tennessee twang and the hair too big and too blonde.
God only knew when I might take to handling snakes in
the faculty lounge.

I knew Jesus' insistence to his followers that . . . *you do not
belong to the world*. . . . But Jesus had never been a blonde,
Southern graduate student in a postmodern department
of a university in postmodern New England. I was more
than willing to belong to that world, if only I could sink
into the backdrop and fit in. I learned to furrow my brow

and make dark, cynical comments in many-syllabled words whose definitions, quite frankly, I was fuzzy on. Shoving bright cotton florals to the back of my closet, I learned to wear colors that we writers and scholars prefer: black and anything resembling rotted olives.

I tried waving away my colleagues' and professors' fears by implying they were *way behind, Sugar,* on their thinking about the revamped nature of the New South—and that they'd read far too much Faulkner.

Come to think of it, I may have, *golly,* forgotten to mention a few points of my own past: for example, that Sand Mountain, the next ridge over from my childhood home, Signal Mountain, was an international hub for snake-handling Baptists. Had my colleagues or professors in grad school come right out and asked, I could have told them there was—*okay, yes, in fact*—a Baptist church in my hometown that rewarded High Attendance Sunday participants by having the pastor lie prostrate, there by the main highway that cut over our mountain, while watermelons were sliced on his stomach.

But nobody asked specifically, so I didn't offer.

I liked to think of myself then, in my twenties and early thirties, as a broad-minded, world-wise, breathtakingly tolerant, ecumenical Christian, though my doctoral program friends and professors kept latching onto the horrors they'd heard, the *Baptist* and the *minister* and the *Southerner* thing, and could not let go.

The truth is, all English department types are a little bit odd, a condition deep-seated in childhood. It all comes, as my friend Betsy put it, from our spending school recesses on the edge of the field reading, never joining in the games of Red Rover, and never developing proper social skills.

Many of us graduate students were closet writers as well, novelists and poets shocked to discover that the world doesn't feel it owes any writer a living. Finding a job wrapped up in words, even if they came chained to a grade book, seemed the closest way to become the starving artists, light on the starving, that we revered.

But even among the admittedly odd, I see now, I stood out as colossally strange.

So I worked harder at sounding sophisticated and urbane and avoiding scary five-letter words like *Jesus*—and I also mashed down my big hair.

I longed to appear smart, or at least not as irredeemably stupid as my East Tennessee accent might daily suggest.

Daily, I failed.

Our department's sixteenth-century literature expert was a person of no declared personal faith, so far as I knew, but she'd reached the end of her patience with postmodern ignorance of anything even remotely Judeo-Christian. Without at least some kind of vague knowledge of the Old and New Testaments, much of the intricate literature she taught made as much sense as long division to a people who'd never learned to count.

Her frustration boiled over into fury one afternoon in a seminar on Edmund Spenser's *The Faerie Queene*. She began pacing the room. Our heads ducked, we pretended to pour over the poem.

"All right, then," she said, clearly disgusted with us. "Answer Spenser's central question from Book One, stanza 38: 'What franticke fit,' quoth he, 'hath thus distraught / Thee, foolish man, so rash a doom to give? / What justice ever other judgment taught, / But he should die, who merites not to live?'"

The professor waited. In silence.

"Spenser is asking here," she spoke slowly, enunciating too carefully, as one does to preschoolers and the very stupid, "who merits not to live?"

More silence.

She began lunging now from one desk to the next. "Tell me, who deserves to die?"

A bearded poet named Brad valiantly lifted his head from the trenches where the rest of us cowered, still keeping our heads down. "The character Despair does, clearly, because he . . ."

Brad the gentle poet was squashed like a bearded bug.

"*Not* the point. What *is* Spenser's point?"

Another student mustered the courage to meet the professor's eye. "Well, the juxtaposition of Despair with Redcrosse knight demonstrates how the latter does *not* deserve to die. He is thus far in the text without flaw and therefore. . . ."

The professor's face had gone eggplant. "No!"

"But . . ."

"*No!*"

"Clearly, then, it's . . ."

"*NO!*"

In exasperation, the professor whirled on me. "Who merits not to live?" she snarled.

It was Sunbeams that saved me just then.

As an adult, I'd taken three years' worth of courses in systematic theology, epistemology, and how to calculate a church's educational space square footage, but like anyone who once was a faithful five-year-old Sunbeam, or ate even a week's worth of Vacation Bible School wafers and watered-down juice, I learned all I really needed to know to answer this question from flannel graphs and quavery-voiced saints who set us on their knees to recite John 3:16. In small, grubby hands, we clutched silken scarves they loaned us to dance, and we sang as we twirled and they plunked a piano:

Come thou fount of every blessing,
Tune my heart to sing thy praise. . . .

The question of who deserves to die, right here, right now, in pain and wretchedness, all our ugliest deeds spelled out in big red letters across our chests, was one drilled into us Sunbeams.

"Everyone," I whispered. My old shyness and a desperate desire to sound like, look like, *be* like, all the awfully smart people around me had me by the throat, and I thought I would strangle to death right there on the cold linoleum floor.

The professor stalked to my desk. "*What* did you say?"

I opened my mouth wider, but the words came out with the volume turned off, so I looked like a big-mouth bass flopped out of the pond. I tried again: "Everyone. Everyone deserves to die."

"*What?*"

"All. . . ." I could hear in my head the words that wanted to trail on its heels: "have sinned and fall short of the glory of God." But I stopped on the *All*. That was plenty to set the whole seminar staring.

The professor's face was inches from mine. For a moment, I saw Sergeant Carter bellowing the *I can't HE-E-E-EAR you* in Gomer Pyle's face.

"*WHY?*" she demanded. I think perhaps she was shouting, but that might have been the proximity of my ear to her mouth. "Why *not* simply succumb to suicide as Despair suggests? *Why* are we not all already dead if that's what we deserve?"

"Well. . . ." This wasn't much more of a mumble.

"Yes?" She paced there in front of my desk waiting for my answer.

"Grace," I croaked.

"Again!"

"*Grace.*"

"*Louder!*"

"*GRACE!*"

"Definition?"

I took a deep breath.

Now, the whole reason a person becomes a writer is that you realize one day that you are orally challenged. The thoughts in your head don't transfer to your tongue like other people's. That with thoughts but no laptop or pen, you are a leopard with spots but no legs.

Had I been able just then to write down my answer, I might have said that grace is what shows up every time before you do to meet you. Grace is a ferocious, arms-open, tears-flowing, bathrobe flapping and slippers flying off into the field kind of love that races toward you from way down the road when you come heading home from being a jerk and a cad and a pig.

Grace, I might have scrawled on my desk, is the fist in the face that you wait for, that you so richly deserve, and the big bone-crushing hug that you're given instead.

But I was expected to speak. So for the out-loud definition, I settled only for this: "Grace: God's . . . favor. God's . . . abundant mercy."

"How do you earn it?"

"You . . . can't. You can't earn it."

"But who deserves it?"

"No one deserves it. Not . . . one of us. It's . . . grace."

Arms crossed, her face purple with rage, the professor spun on her heel, stalked to the opposite end of the room, wheeled to face us again, and stood there.

We held our collective scholarly breath.

Then this, her final word hurled at our heads: "*Yes.*"

That was her benediction.

My friend Brad-the-bearded-poet patted me on the arm as we all stumbled from class. "There for a moment," he whispered, "I thought we'd all be eaten for lunch."

"Sunbeams," I said, nodding.

"What?"

"Never mind."

That day, I drove home through a blizzard clogging the traffic on the Mass Pike out of Boston to a pitiful trickle.

On that day of the *Faerie Queene* seminar, Book One, and the beginnings of a blizzard, I sang to the beat of my windshield wipers straining under the weight of wet snow, and I could see five-year-old Sunbeams dancing with silk scarves, twirling and laughing, the soft colors floating over our heads as our arms lifted and swayed:

O, to grace how great a debtor
Daily I'm constrained to be,
Let thy goodness like a fetter
Bind my wandering heart to thee. . . .

I was learning then, and continue to learn, that there is a deep wisdom that transcends the sea of knowledge—right through the ocean floor to the earth's center, to life's core, and death's.

These days, the walls of my home are lined with books, not leather-bound trophies but tattered paperbacks mostly. I like to think they suggest to visitors at least an appearance of wisdom, years of late-night reading. More likely they suggest years of minimal income, and my being severely decorator-challenged.

I asked my own students today—now that I'm the pacing professor—to name the wisest person they knew.

An artistic free spirit spoke up first, naming with a wry grin a high-ranking American politician. The class, products of a politically cynical generation like mine, laughed. No one attempted to defend his suggestion, not even the young woman whose father campaigned for that politician. She, in fact, spoke next, naming her father, a former celebrity NASCAR driver, as her definition of wisdom. Another student added to that quickly, naming her mother. The name of a high school teacher came after that. So it went.

Granted, they're young still, and don't number among the people they "know" the great and famous minds of our time. And they're too honest, God bless them, to have sunk to brownnosing and naming the professor who would within days be assigning them final grades.

There's wisdom in who they've found wise thus far in their lives: the loving, the nurturing, the teaching, and the caring. Those whom they've seen live out what they've learned.

If I am wiser now than I was in early graduate school, it's less because of the books we devoured back then or since, blessed books, than because of that other learning that comes only with the passage of years, blessed fine lines of aging. Learning to live into mercy. Understanding the days we thought we'd been faithful, and weren't. Seeing the good we should have made time for, the scything of words never meant to hurt anyone. Finding ourselves finally grown into a daily communion with grace.

Saint Augustine, a fourth-century professor of rhetoric, who'd been, by his own vivid description, a lusty, self-obsessed young man, developed not only a thirst for knowledge but also a thirst for God. In his supremely honest *Confessions*, he writes first of an intellectual but not a heart conversion. Then one day he heard the voice of a child pointing him toward Scripture, and instructing him, "Take it and read."

Often, the wisdom of the winding-on years brings us back to the faith of a child. *Let the little children come to me,* Jesus scolded his disciples, *because they get it in ways you people have not.* All three synoptic Gospels recount Jesus' rebuke to his followers and embrace of the kids. *You wanna know what God wants from you?* Jesus demands. *Well, take a look.* The writer Luke quotes Jesus as suggesting that unless we catch a clue and become like children, we haven't got an icicle's chance in the tropics of knowing God.

It's a childlike openness, after all, that can understand how we've misunderstood altogether: who and what we're about. That we've mistaken information for wisdom.

This summer our little family of five will heap ourselves into a boxy blue van and pilgrimage to New England, where we'll observe the twenty-fifth reunion of my husband's graduating class from Harvard. Together, we'll stroll the children through Harvard Yard and then perhaps down Quincy Street to pause in front of Emerson Hall. Here, my husband, Todd, will recount for his captive audience the debate over which of two inscriptions Emerson's facade would eventually bear. The debate ran between these two lines: "Man Is the Measure of All Things" from the ancient Greek philosopher Protagoras and "What Is Man That Thou Art Mindful of Him . . . ?" from Psalm 8. We will explain for the younger children how these are very different ways of seeing our own capabilities, and our place and purpose in the universe. Then our middle school daughter will crane her neck and shoot us that oldest-child, slightly superior smile to say she sees who won the debate: a carved-stone record of arrogance bowing to mystery.

Much as it disturbs me most days to admit it, in a world where framed diplomas and grand, glittering displays of achievements open doors and turn heads, the way of the Cross runs roughshod over résumés, deep-sixes curriculum vitae, and is no respecter of brilliant bio sketches. In fact, the goal, in terms of learning more of an extravagant grace and an inexplicable peace, seems to be backward mobility: becoming like children. Without pretense or arrogance. Without apologies for who we are, or long to be.

Please know: I cherish learning, celebrate it as a path out of dead ends for at-risk youth, and like to think that once in a while I help crowbar a window to a wider world for my own students, just as my professors daily did for me. Yet my own life and culture demonstrate daily that while knowledge may lead to wisdom, they are not—*so* not—the same thing.

As for me, I still owe a great debt to Sunbeams.

Because sometimes, even in our clever efforts to appear smart, or to blend in with the world, wisdom still finds us out. We have no choice but to confess what we know to be true: *Here's who I am, here's WHY I am.* And then hold close the *YES* that no one deserves, not one. It's grace.

5 Holiness

"Holiness," said Walter Rauschenbusch, "is goodness on fire." This captures well the holiness—and the danger—of Jesus, his power to attract and disturb, and even to destroy, before re-creation or redemption can occur. Just as fire itself draws us to its light, its warmth, its wild beauty, its power. Pulls us to circle around it, watch it crackle and consume, even as it reminds us of our own wan endeavors, our weakness.

Most of us, along with our culture, create some tamer, more easily contained version of Jesus and the holiness he represents. A Jesus who becomes easy to laugh at, shrug off, dismiss. Part of our one-dimensional embrace. A type. Not a person, not the living God who speaks and rattles the foundations of the earth.

Accounts of Jesus' life depict his regular rebukes—his goodness on fire—of his culture's religious authorities, those who played overtime with legalisms but fumbled compassion. In these stories, Jesus sometimes sounds as if he's arrived to rid the world of all rules, all rigid commandments, all moral bars to leap over. Then, in place of an obstacle course of regulations divinely designed to trip us up, Jesus offers forgiveness and mercy.

But his mercy actually raises the bar. Ratchets up all the rules from our low-threshold "Shalt-Nots" to new standards entirely. Jesus gives us, not behavioral checks, but heart-expectations. Here, Jesus tells us, is how people live in grace, and hunger after the wild beauty of the holy.

While the church often belabors the "Don'ts," "binding with briars [our] joys and desires," as William Blake wrote, we long to grow hearts after God's heart. To move past No, and live into Yes.

Just as we're checking off boxes down a long, dreary list of the bad we've not—or mostly not—done, we hear Jesus explaining from across the room, on the far side of the punch bowl, *You've heard it was said . . . long ago, 'You shall not murder,' . . . But I tell you that anyone who is angry with a brother or sister will be subject to judgment. . . .* And Jesus goes on from there, leaving no cobwebbed corner of our insides unseen: Lust. Selfishness. Deceit. Revenge. Greed. Pettiness. Pride.

Suddenly, it's not enough to refrain from committing an officially off-limits offense. Instead, it's all about where our thoughts wandered, our gazes shifted, our intentions slipped.

And suddenly, we're in very deep trouble.

I wouldn't venture to say this about you, but it turns out I'm not a very nice person. Not in the way Jesus defines this business of becoming "holy as God is holy."

Holiness as our culture defines it doesn't look hip or attractive. Like *Saturday Night Live's* Church Lady, in drag with a fake Southern accent, this cultural holiness is prim, petty, and shocked, *shocked* at all forms of misbehavior, from coloring outside the lines to corporate fraud.

And holiness as defined by a long list of checked off "Shalt-Nots" is no better. Clarence Jordan, author of *The Cottonpatch Gospels*, said living according to legalism was like chaining a mad dog to a tree and calling it a good dog because it never bit anybody.

Religion, merely religion, is leashing the snarling, frothing parts of ourselves and hoping nobody steps in too close to see what we are.

Holiness, real holiness, the kind Jesus presents, is not about chains or checklists but hunger. And longing. Finding ourselves desperate for meaning, for purpose, for something bigger and richer and beyond the tawdry this-world that we let define us. Wishing to wipe down the slates of our pasts, clean up our acts, start over again. To live this time for something higher and wider and deeper. More wild. More dangerous. More destructive and creative. More holy.

One of the best sermons I've ever heard—and I've heard too many—was by Julie Pennington-Russell, who spoke of purity not as an absence of mistakes and misdeeds, or as innocence that never has shaken hands with experience, but as a single-minded pursuit of God. That's holiness. The Jesus definition, not the cultural one.

Our own unsullied state, or not, is no longer the point.

Because the fire of real holiness burns up the past. Refines it. Makes way for rebuilding, for growth, for beginning again.

Jesus calls us to holiness past our own sin, our own screw-ups, our delusions that we were doing just fine, thanks, on that checklist of "Don'ts." But part of what must be consumed by his fire is our shame. Not just what we've done or left undone, but what's been done *to* us. The woundedness we've worn as our own skin, and called ourselves dirty, disgusting, despicable.

Some of us learn about holiness through what we know about the sullied state, learn about purity through shame. It makes no sense that we could come to know holiness, the living God, by excavating the dead, carefully hidden parts of ourselves. Yet Jesus calls out to what's been forced on us, and the fires of goodness, of holiness, burn away the lie we'd put on and belted and buckled: that we're ruined, sullied, worthless.

Whenever I've been in a group of women who've become comfortable enough with one another to speak openly, and vulnerably, if something comes up about any past sexual violence, I'm thunderstruck every time at the percentages. In one creative writing class I taught, three of the eight women had been raped. More had been molested. One, raped at age ten, channeled her pain into a novel, writing eloquently, heart-wrenchingly, of the attack of the main character as if a bull were charging the child—*because that's how it felt,* she told us—the animal snorting and pawing the child's red skirt into shreds floating into the air, the bull trampling out her innocence.

My own story wasn't nearly so horrific—yet I understood the maimed innocence. I was sixteen and finishing dressing in the upstairs locker room of our high school gym. As usual, I was running late for the next class, probably because I'd been talking faster than showering or dumping baby powder down a sweaty back. When the door opened at the foot of the stairs, I assumed it was a female coach come to crack a well-deserved whip.

But the face that appeared in the door wasn't female at all. It was a workman, presumably in the building to change a lightbulb or splice a wire. Or not.

He marched directly to where I stood, frozen.

Before that day, I'd been dubious about stories of people who are molested and later claim that they were paralyzed with fear and horror, and never technically said that key word NO. From the outside looking in, it sounded preposterous: *What, so you didn't scream, didn't kick his lights out?*

Ever since that day, though, I've believed them all: all the stories of paralysis and horror like handcuffs binding your arms down to your sides. All the nightmares of trying to run from the monster and your feet won't lift from the pavement, because when the monster approached me, and then put a hand on me, I did not move. I could only feel the nausea moving from my stomach to my throat, feel my throat close shut in a scream that never would rise

Here's what he said, his hand on me: "*Shame.*" Long and drawn out, that word was. *SHAME.* And with his face in mine, he grinned.

I remember it as a brown grin, full of half-rotted, tobacco-stained teeth, not all of them present. That may have been the case, or I may have added the bad teeth in my memory because good dental hygiene didn't fit with my remembrance of a monster.

SHAME, he said, through brown, grinning teeth.

And shame is indeed what I felt. Not the fury I surely *should* have felt at the time. Not the rage. Instead, the message I received, and held close, was that this had been my fault. Something about me that had made him think he could do this, some serious deficiency in me that had kept me from screaming for help, or knocking him senseless.

And then he left, walking out of the locker room calmly, as if he knew his one word would seal my lips forever. As if proving he'd wounded me with a touch just as surely as if he'd swung a bat at my head. I was as stunned and without sense.

Another girl appeared from the showers, her mouth hanging open. Maybe he'd heard her approach and that was why he'd left.

She was a tall girl, pretty and athletic, one who'd been of the popular set in her middle school years but who'd become, for reasons I never knew, coarser and rougher by high school, and maybe it was that shift that put people off. I wonder now what it was in her own life that changed her. I do remember her eyes locking on mine, and I recall thinking that in that moment she both wondered at my not screaming for help and also understood somehow why I hadn't. She shouted a single obscenity down the stairwell after him. I recall being grateful for that.

We stood then and stared at each other, the two of us scared and sixteen—and I suspect, though I'll never know for sure about her—both of us sullied. Both of us wounded.

We never said anything at all to each other. Perhaps because, given my state of mind, there was nothing to say. She never asked if I was going to report him to the school authorities or tell my parents. It was clear, I suppose, if I hadn't been able to so much as swat his hand away or claw his eyes out or kick him crippled, I wouldn't march any time soon into the principal's office. And who would believe me, anyway, that I'd done nothing to stop him, not run to hide, not found the obscenity she'd been able to hurl at the back of his head? No one, I knew. Because it was *my* shame.

Stains and dirt and woundedness. *Shame.*

But here's what can happen:

Holiness—real purity—can come along and stretch out a hand, wounded itself, and shame loses its grip. Because holiness is not the absence of past shame, or of genuine guilt. Holiness is not having never screwed up royally in the past. Having not screamed when you should have. Or having said all the wrong things when you should have kept your mouth shut.

Holiness, according to Jesus, is never about the sordidness or stupidity or self-delusion of where we've been. Holiness doesn't sit still to be strapped down by what we've done, what we've left undone, or what's been done to us. It's about where we're headed right now. The sacred ground where our feet stand this very day. And the path up ahead.

Holiness according to Jesus slashes ties with our pasts. Leaves them there in the dust. Becomes a single-minded pursuit of the purity that is God.

With Jesus, holiness is never about our woundedness but his. How that heals us. And helps us to help others heal.

Sometimes, perhaps, holiness has a soft-pawed entrance, step by step, that is quiet and gradual in our lives. Not the bright release of shame, but another kind of encounter with Jesus.

One day last summer, I'd been asked to write an on-line devotion about the twelfth chapter of Romans. The words *cling to what is good, be devoted, joyful, patient, faithful, keep your spiritual fervor serving* were bumping around in my head as I looked up from my stack of books and my laptop to see the general manager of the restaurant where I'd set up office that morning. It occurred to me that I'd read somewhere calculations of how much money that restaurant chain loses each year by choosing not to be open on Sundays, and it struck me as a helpful statistic. Years ago,

I'd met the corporation's founder, and had been intrigued by his business philosophies, and his enormous financial support of at-risk children.

So I asked the general manager about how much money they lose.

"Nothing," the general manager said.

"But—."

"Nothing."

They're a strikingly kind, friendly bunch at this restaurant franchise, so it seemed unlikely he was just brushing me off to get back to his ledgers. I tried one last time: "Surely you—."

"Because you can't lose," he went on, "what you shouldn't have had in the first place."

Turns out this is their corporate way of explaining much of their business practice.

There's something here of what the apostle Paul is trying to say about the journey to holiness when he instructs, *cling to the good, be joyful, be faithful, be not conformed to this world.* Operating one's business on Sunday may not be evil, granted; but making our decisions in relation to Christ's leading us to think and to add and to subtract and to balance our checkbooks and corporate accounts insists on emphatically clinging to the good in a material way. This is spiritual practice. *Doing* theology.

Here's an idea that flies in the face of how the world does math. It's a lesson I'd like to remember: *You can't lose what you shouldn't have had in the first place.*

One of those little step-stones of simple wisdom. Ungussied-up goodness on a long road to holiness.

My songwriter friend Kyle Matthews once composed lyrics he assumed no one would ever hear outside his own home, because the chorus spoke of our failures as unspiritual beings with yearnings for spiritual truth. Which was, perhaps, precisely why the song hit the top-forty charts. Its lyrics describe an ordinary man passing monastery walls each day and longing to know what the monks inside, surely closer to God, know about the spiritual path that the man doesn't. When the man finally has the chance to approach one of the brothers, he's at first disillusioned by the monk's too-simple confession:

We fall down. We get up.
We fall down. We get up.
And the saints are just the sinners
Who fall down, and get up.

Far from the inner-circle secret the man had hoped to secure.

Yet that's where our hope lies. That even serious stumbles—our own or others' that took us down with them—do not block the road to holiness forever. That Jesus does not turn away in disgust from our bloodied falls.

Which is where spiritual practice comes in.

The practice of spiritual disciplines can be the picks and ropes that help us keep to the path. Help us climb. Not earning our own way in a hand-over-hand climb, but putting forth some effort toward growth, toward moving forward on the path. Not working our own way to the land of the righteous elite, but a gut-grateful response to Jesus' open-armed invitation to beginning again.

I've been slow in learning this lesson. Open-armed invitation or not. Raised in a cheery, chatty Christian tradition, I memorized the order of the Old Testament prophets not for divine reward but for material bribes. In my church tradition, moments of quiet in worship occurred only when someone forgot to flip on the podium's mike. I'd been well-schooled in the importance of Scripture and community and commitment to Jesus, and of cheese grits casseroles and sweet tea brewed fresh every day. I loved the church of my childhood—still do. But we chatty, cheery disciples didn't go in for silence or fasting.

My first real attempt at these, in fact, sprang from self-interest.

As a minister on staff at my church in Cambridge, I'd initiated the summer weekend retreat, which, year after year, I began dreading. Despite my intending to provide opportunities of profound spiritual enlightenment, something always went wrong with our food orders: mountains of watery cole slaw and only one little bowl of baked beans for a whole horde of hungry pilgrims. Or there were too many workshops to choose from, or too few. The main speaker left too little room for participants to commune with each other. Or the retreat's structure left too much free time. And no one ever remembered a Frisbee.

One year, I rebelled. Exhausted and harried in my own life and surrounded by people who looked and behaved almost as badly, I longed to be shut away from well-meaning critique.

I wanted nothing whatsoever to do with cole slaw. Ever again.

Thus began the retreat of Prayer, Silence, and Fasting (Especially from Cole Slaw), birthed by a church-weary curmudgeon.

All of us staggered about that weekend, bleary-eyed from imagined starvation, glancing at watches—*had it really been only an hour since that final meal?*—and smiling shyly at one another when we passed from one secluded spot to another—*are we allowed to smile a hello while practicing silence?* While I don't remember that weekend as a breakthrough of medieval mystic proportions, I do recall that when we finally did end our silence, the small group I was in spoke about our own spiritual journeys—and lack thereof—as openly and honestly as any I'd ever heard.

Somehow, silence and solitude enriched what followed: community.

Just as the practice of spiritual disciplines helps us live into holiness.

It smacked of contradiction to me then, and still does. But for many of us, the retreat marked another step in the journey, more tools for the climb.

Sometimes a path toward holiness—and with holiness—can be a simple and honest, even if poorly motivated, faithful trekking forward. A recognition that the journey toward holiness requires steps on our part. Sometimes steps that highlight the *un*holy.

Among my circle of friends, I'm aware of only one who has fasted for any length: thirty days straight. Stephanie was in Uganda, and intent on letting her thirty-day fast be not "simply starving oneself," but focused on prayer. The journal she kept during her fast reveals how spiritual discipline well-practiced first exposes the *un*holy: by day four, she recalls, "I thought I was going to die. I was so miserable, grouchy, irritable, not liking any person who came near me, having severe leg cramps. . . ."

By day eleven, she wrote:

> Sensing the evil in my heart, silence, pondering, wishing, wanting, feeling very *un*spiritual, weakness, sweetness, eating the Scriptures. . . . Joints aching, and I've had a bit of pain behind the eyes. . . . So many things in my heart that I ask God to change—greed, impatience, hatred, selfishness, irritation, laziness, rebellion. I am at the point that I know I cannot change myself. LORD HAVE MERCY.

Nearing day thirty, she recorded in her journal:

> I am looking wasted—like the catatonic people I used to care for in the hospital. It hurts to sit too long on a hard surface . . . There are short periods every day when I feel very hungry and empty but for the most

part, I'm fine and able to concentrate. At least I can usually meditate, pray, think; reading can be a strain after a few hours. I often just want silence, and spend many hours outside sitting. . . . The insects and birds make a lot of wonderful noise. We talk of food a lot and I miss it so much. . . . The desire for marriage and to be with a man is consuming—I do thank God for such desires but pray they would not rule over me. Men who fast say that there is a period in which lust comes calling. . . . I pray God will keep my heart in a place of thankfulness and gratitude, whether I am with little or with plenty.

Sometimes, as Stephanie's journal reflects, quietness and discipline and God's mercy let us glimpse the mess and muck in ourselves. Which becomes, ironically, the most important step in any stumbling journey toward the holy.

In some seasons of life, we need to hear judgment in addition to grace, need shaking up and setting straight. Here, holiness can arrive with smash and roar, with a force that takes out some of the furniture and gashes the walls.

If evil can be a bull, then surely holiness can be a lion.

Jesus was the one who sent tables flying when he found people in the courts of the temple taking advantage of the low-income crowd. The one who rips into the self-righteous. The ungrateful. Self-focused. Distracted. The people who look like me many days.

The gospel accounts of Jesus highlight his compassion, but also his harshness. Whenever we jettison Jesus the Ultimate

Judge in favor of Jesus the Divine Surfer Dude, we're not reading closely enough. We're deluding ourselves.

Sometimes God's love for us, God's judgment, can arrive with its own thunder. That thunder, that call to holiness, can take the strangest of forms. Like a woman whose feet are planted and fists are curled, whose voice rises above the dull rumble of life. Take, for instance, an evening with Ginger and Kay.

These two friends and I get together for a weekend retreat on a nearly annual basis: grown women giggling hysterically in the back corner booth of a restaurant where the hostess, after taking one look at us, wisely stashed us. We met more than two decades ago—which is odd, we assure one other, since none of us looks a day over twenty. Through years of relocations and families and academic degrees and job changes, we've met to moan over the young adult years that we shared, and misspent, and sometimes we cry over the present and then dream of the future.

Holiness is not the word that first comes to mind when we three get together.

But follow the three of us in a riverside stroll, and witness a prophetic juggernaut. At least one of us is the call-to-account thunder and crash. The other two of us duck for cover and claim not to know her.

One girlfriend-getaway weekend landed us in San Antonio, Texas. Now in order to traverse a certain part of the city's spectacular River Walk, one must walk through a restaurant-sports bar kind of place that I won't name but that starts that with an H and whose name sort of rhymes with Losers, or Looters. This Certain Restaurant, which hires waitresses with only certain sorts of body shapes, is not my favorite place. I don't suppose it's a newsflash that Certain Restaurants are demeaning to women, insisting on their waitresses wearing their shirts too tight and shorts that think they're a belt. And *pantyhose* with their shorts? Please.

Two of the three of us friends are fairly soft-spoken, prone, if anything, to erring on the side of keeping our mouths shut too often. The third of us errs—if, in fact, she ever errs—on the side of frankness. As we strolled together down the River Walk and were forced by its course straight through this Certain Restaurant's outdoor seating, it was the third of us who planted her feet in the middle of the vortex of swirling platters and flexing biceps and undulating hips in orange nylon, painfully short shorts. Two of us ducked our heads and kept walking, fearing what was next. The third placed her hands on her hips.

"Here it comes," two of us muttered, walking away faster, tucking our chins deeper down in our collars.

And come it did.

"THIS PLACE," the third of the three of us blasted the crowd, who paused in their ogling and their wiping barbeque sauce from their jowls. "THIS PLACE IS SETTING WOMEN BACK THREE HUNDRED YEARS!"

The Certain Restaurant grew quiet, outdoors and indoors, drool and barbeque sauce both dripping from dropped lower jaws. Orange nylon hushed its *shhh, shhh.*

Forks clattered to a stop on ceramic plates. Frosted mugs thudded down onto lacquered tabletops. All eyes swung to the planted feet and hands on hips.

To the prophet. In lip gloss and capris.

One friend and I kept walking, heads down.

Much as I hurried to separate myself from the storm that broke on the heads of the poor unsuspecting barflies that night, it's what I wanted to say. Not a tirade against how much skin was showing or who shacked up with whom— that was never the point. It was—and is—about what I see sometimes in my own life. The outrage of aiming only for someone else's approval. Judging our own worth by the glint or the indifference in someone's glance at us. Believing our purpose could be defined by anyone other than the God who crafted us in the womb.

The truth is, Jesus might have said something of the same thing as my fiery friend, Ginger, had he been strolling down the River Walk with us that night.

And I'd have run for cover then, too.

Scripture paints Jesus as never standing for women being tagged with how they look or how they don't, or what man left them standing there holding the bedsheet. And he takes on men—the screwups, the arrogant, the disabled, the despairing, the cheats—with the same compassion and mercy and matter-of-fact expectation of living out of the labels we've let be sewn onto our souls. That we would live into holiness.

And Jesus challenges us to help each other along in this task of holiness.

Which is where three women come in, or any faith community's insistence that we not settle for mediocre marriages or mediocre friendships or mediocre spiritual lives. Holiness lives in those places, even those storms, where we're called back home to God.

Holiness is something I stumbled upon while reading the late short story writer Andre Dubus. A big man and former Marine, he'd been side-swiped by a car on a Massachusetts interstate while helping a woman stranded by the side of road. He lost the use of both legs. Dubus, a devout Catholic, wrote powerfully of what his learning to live in a wheelchair had taught him on a spiritual plane.

Whether or not you or I end up anytime soon in a wheelchair, or ever, perhaps it helps to be reminded we're all in the same boat—or chair—whether we know it or not, never so invincible as we think, never so eternally capable as we'd like to appear. All we can really ever count on for sure: the simple *You don't know what tomorrow will bring . . . or even today. So lean harder on Jesus.*

We all live, I'm reminded these days, by Andre Dubus, with great gifts and with real limitations.

We learn that both rigid, rule-based religion and cheap, easy grace leave us restless, hollow, and mean.

We find ourselves longing. And listening. Maybe for the first time.

And if we're paying attention, we hear Jesus call us out from where real judgment left us ready for change.

Past legalisms. Past all our whining excuses.

Past all our shame. Past all our pasts.

Jesus calls us to a place that is hard sometimes and beautiful.

To goodness that is dangerous. Destructive and re-creative.

To passion that upends our plans for security, and points us instead toward peace.

Holiness. All of us holding onto each other, wounded and healed and healing, together in the outstretched arms of our God.

6 Peace

A few years ago, our whole family decided to march for a cause in which we passionately believed—actually, to march against a cause in which we passionately did not. It was the kids' first protest of any sort, and our oldest daughter, Julia, was elated, primarily because she was an eight-year-old who thought deeply about things, and partly, I suspect, because there were TV cameras everywhere.

Julia carried a sign she'd designed herself that read, in big, bold, hand-lettered blue magic marker:

"Love Your Enemies"
—Jesus

A number of people in the crowd beamed at her, or patted her on the shoulder. Things were going well, it was clear. I turned to chat with a friend I'd just spotted.

When I turned back to where Julia was standing just a few feet away, I found her talking with a man I'd never seen before. That is, she was listening to him as she backed toward me. Bending down close to her face and shaking his finger at her, he pointed to the sign she'd so carefully crafted.

"An enemy," he scolded her, "is only someone we've never met. We assume he is an enemy because we do not know him. But if we knew him, he would not be an enemy. . . . " It went on from there, enough edge to his voice that I stepped up beside Julia and dropped an arm over her shoulders.

Maybe the man had a point: I didn't know him at all—only that he was scaring my daughter. And though we were theoretically on the same side of this march, his making my daughter cower was making him a good candidate for my enemy. I didn't know him, and I really, *really* didn't like him.

It occurred to me to tell him that I agreed about having no enemies on one level, but that also he'd just become mine.

I thought of the sign my daughter had crafted. The passage her sign quoted was bad enough, this bit of loving one's enemies, but the context is even more bizarre:

> You have heard that it was said, "Love your neighbor and hate your enemy." But I tell you, love your enemies and pray for those who persecute you, that you may be children of your Father in heaven. He causes the sun to rise on the evil and the good, and sends rain on the righteous and the unrighteous.

If you love those who love you, what reward will you get?
Are not even the tax collectors doing that? And if you greet
only your own people, what are you doing more than others?
Do not even pagans do that? Be perfect, therefore, as your
heavenly Father is perfect.

There goes Jesus raising the bar again with his *You've*
heard it said . . . but I tell you. The passage openly admits
the existence of people who are, simply, evil. Those we
have every reason to hate—every right to despise both
their methods and their madness. And yet, Jesus insists,
it's not enough simply to refrain from giving them the
violent, suffering end they deserve. Go further. Find a way
to pray to God for their good—for their transformation,
and maybe your own.

It's Jesus' outrageous instructions that guide the apostle
Paul's words when he quotes the book of Proverbs:

If your enemy is hungry, feed him;
if he is thirsty, give him something to drink.
In doing this you will heap burning coals on his head.
Do not be overcome by evil, but overcome evil with good.

But here's what I find comforting, despite the unreasonable
demands of Jesus' life, and of Paul's words, and of that sign
my daughter carried: There's an assumption here that we
do, like it or not, have enemies in this world.

Forget the sweet, Up-with-People assumption that if we
just come to know someone well enough, they'll become
our friend. I believed that when I was seventeen at youth

camp, all of us safe and snuggly and warm by a campfire that crackled and soothed, all of us high on s'mores and hormones and campfire smoke inhalation. Most of us focused a little on *Let there be peace on earth and let it begin with me,* but far more on the precise melt and char of our marshmallows.

But what Scripture tells us to expect from the world is that there simply *will* be people who disagree with us, and violently so. There will be people we find revolting. There will be people who detest us for no reason. And some who despise us because we've given them good reason.

What Jesus makes uncomfortably clear is that the job ahead, peace, is not for the passive. We're not to be of the chameleon class of people who agree with everyone they meet in the frantic hope of offending no one. Rather, we're to be people of principle. But it's not enough to simply decide we don't like someone's face, or what some past run-in with "their type" has made us resent. It might be human to land here, but we're called to move on from that place:

Live in harmony with one another. Do not be proud but be willing to associate with people of low position. Do not think you are superior.

Do not repay anyone evil for evil. Be careful to do what is right in the eyes of everyone. If it is possible, as far as it depends on you, live at peace with everyone. Do not take revenge, my dear friends, but leave room for God's wrath, for it is written: "it is mine to avenge; I will repay," says the Lord.

These are verses I'm uneasy with, being someone who seethes well. Left to my inclinations, if Jesus would leave me alone, I'm a champion grudge holder. My Italian husband is descended from the artistically gifted, passionate people who gave us that wonderful word *vendetta*. Though having none of their dark hair or fine olive skin, they're my people in this one way: *vendetta* is a word I can sink my teeth into. Especially if you're scaring my daughter.

But Jesus sets out a different path. And the apostle Paul, who'd once taken his own dislikes and religious differences to the point of securing death warrants, feels his way along Jesus' path. In the passage above, Paul maps out Jesus' road to peace: one that doesn't ask us to put up with abuse, but also—and here's where the going gets tough—one in which there's no stop for revenge on the journey. No retaliation allowed. None. Except for this one: God knows our leanings toward pettiness—so that in feeding our enemy, and extending concern, we're somehow getting a kind of godly vengeance in knowing that maybe our enemy will end up feeling small, and wrong, and maybe even more petty than we do. There's comfort, you know, in that.

Even here, there's a nod toward the reality that we'll feel mistreated or misunderstood or enraged by someone's or some group's behavior. In this world we *will* have enemies, despite all the marshmallows and campfire songs in the world. But then Jesus calls us to do the outlandish: to love our enemies anyway, to be aggressors for goodness and harmony among people who, if they're like us, might not always, or *ever,* be deserving of love.

Peace according to Jesus is not the state of feeling safe and secure and undisturbed by conflict. Which doesn't sound like good news for me, by nature part of the Peace-At-All-Costs crowd.

It's been my personality type, I'm ashamed to admit, who have throughout history pleaded with those who feel unjustly treated to *just lower your voice, go a little more slowly, be patient, don't upset anyone.* It was the Peace-At-All-Costs crowd that Martin Luther King Jr. blasted in his "Letter from a Birmingham Jail" as being worse than the Klan in terms of impeding real peace: peace that flows down like waters from justice, not just what stagnates in the absence of conflict. Grown men in white bedsheets with eyeholes are merely ignorant buffoons compared with the deadliness of well-educated, respected citizens and clergy who keep quiet in the face of raging evil.

It was the Peace-At-All-Costs crowd that responded to Harriet Beecher Stowe's *Uncle Tom's Cabin* with pro-slavery novels, many of them including introductions in which the authors begged for an end to the fractious verbal sparring over slavery. They pled for harmony and what these authors called peace, which translated into abolitionists' keeping quiet and letting the status quo quietly reign. For these pro-slavery authors, who often invoked Scripture, Jesus' *Love your enemies* meant simply that their enemies, those speaking against the accepted cultural climate, should put a lid on it.

I'm learning, slowly, that to be a person of peace means far more than being a person who simply despises conflict. There is such a thing as peace out of courage, standing firm in the face of firehoses and oncoming tanks. These peacemakers are the children of God.

False peace can come out of cowardice, or, at the very least, peace out of a desperate neediness for harmony.

Me, I want the lion to lie down with the lamb 24-7, and for them to agree on what kind of pizza they'll have delivered.

I want to live in a world where people say gushing, glowing, glorious things about one another's haircuts and new ties, whether or not it's entirely true. I want people to be aware of each other's differing views on the current nations at war and Presidential campaign front-runners, but not challenge each other at parties or places of worship or work—at least not while I'm in the room. I like my doughnuts *and* conversation frosted in sugar.

I'm learning that part of my yearning for peace is God-driven, and part of it is the pansy ducking for cover.

Which is where God's courage comes in.

When I fail to forgive, or fail to even attempt it. Or even fail to pray that I would *want* to attempt it.

Or when I evade conversations on issues where the differing viewpoints of good-hearted people directly collide.

Years ago in New England, a group of us gathered for discussion after a sermon on war and peace. In the room were represented different nationalities as well as political perspectives, from pacifists, adherents of the Just War Theory, and several members of the United States Navy and Air Force, including one who would soon become the first American woman combat pilot. All of us were people of faith.

The conversation was civil. And thought-provoking. And helpful in knocking flat some of my straw men and stereotypes, and watching that happen for others.

What strikes me as profoundly sad now, though, is that I can point to that day as an exception, a time when people of faith with wildly different perspectives circled their chairs and did not name-call but instead helped each other think about what Jesus might think—about war and modern weaponry and how peace might be achieved.

Perhaps faith communities tend to talk about personal peace in safe, irrelevant-to-daily-life ways precisely because we're afraid. Shaken by Jesus' words and his life. Appalled and hoping that if we squint, that dangerous bit about *Love your enemies* or his words from the cross, *Father, forgive them,* could be read another way. With *revenge* written in plainly between the lines.

Perhaps we suspect the ugly, peeling-paint truth: that there is violence in our own hearts. And that we have only to open our mouths in the presence of people we don't like the looks of, or the voting tendencies of, and out comes the fist-shaking we'd tried to disguise with polite smiles.

Catherine of Siena refers to God as a "pierced wine-barrel," with love overflowing and intoxicating our every impulse. It occurs to me that sometimes in the past, I've not just carried grudges. At times, I've bathed them and clothed them, put ribbons in their hair, fed and raised them to adulthood.

My husband credits this to my writer's memory for dialogue. But it's an ugly trait if you cross me. I'll remember verbatim what you said, what I said, and the pitch of your voice just before you rolled your eyes.

For me, remembering, tending, enshrining every wrong done against me or mine can be painful, and potentially violent. Memory can become destructive, dismantling peace stone upon stone and leaving rubble.

On an individual heart level, peace is something only God can provide. Peace has, surprisingly, little to do with circumstances, with how kind the boss was today or if the kids bickered in the backseat of the car, or whether the Red Sox went to the World Series—important as that is. Peace is the pierced wine-barrel, overflowing all human understanding, which is another way of saying that it will never make sense to us in this life. Not, at least, measured by how our culture pictures peace: investment portfolios, gated communities, or being able to control what our children watch on cable TV. This plastic peace can be blindered contentment, conveniently ignoring the troubles of others. Often, my desire for quiet and stillness is choosing to focus on things that do not disturb me—to see only the dog slobbering sweetly on my feet, the petunias I planted, watered by a wet, wonderful spring.

Jesus' Sermon on the Mount, I once heard Archbishop Desmond Tutu stress, teaches not "Blessed are the peace*lovers*," but "Blessed are the peace*makers*."

Makers is a word with energy and action behind it. More fight than flight.

Peace according to Jesus has to do with the Cross, an act of horrific violence met by aggressive nonviolence, and a power that violence could not overcome. If we see any example of peace in the Cross, then surely it's not that we're to sit still, making daisy chains and hoping that little children won't have their legs blown off by landmines, or their mothers mangled by shells.

Both in our dealings person to person and nation to nation, surely this is where justice comes in, and fairness, making wrong into right: justice falling down in torrents. Bringing peace that flows like fine wine from a bottomless barrel with holes in its sides.

Catherine of Siena also wrote this: "You [God] fill our understanding with joy and light. You flood every memory that's trying to find You, and You leave my heart and soul and mind incapable of remembering, understanding or loving anything other than Yourself, good sweet Jesus, Blood and Fire, ineffable Love!"

I associate blood and fire with war, or tragedy maybe. With the bombing of Dresden. With burned-over villages in Vietnam. With the Twin Towers collapsing in parallel flame. With carnage, human limbs ripped loose from their bodies lying in stacks upon city streets.

But Catherine is speaking of Jesus, whose blood and whose fire heals even as it burns through the blindfolds we'd used to not see. Jesus' fire burns down into the earth where we thought we'd buried our heads. Burns up the unwritten contract of Don't Rock My Boat and I'll Leave Yours Alone. Turns to cinder the armor of civility, good manners, and a graciousness that insists we must not offend one another.

The greatest courage is the outrageous, inflaming insistence that we let go of our grudges and devote passion and money and resources and mobilization behind a ferocious campaign for peace.

Peacemaking, then, can't be pretending our enemies have become our close, personal friends with whom we long to do lunch and coffee. The gospel of Jesus never asks that of us. Becoming people of peace—children of God, as Jesus called it—means learning to live with our enemies in ways that do not contradict the angels' birth announcement for Jesus: *Glory to God in the highest heaven, and on earth peace....*

A businesswoman who serves with me on a committee says her husband describes her modus operandi as being much like a Doberman pinscher's, the only difference between her and the dog being that a Doberman will one day let go. I like this in a woman—if she's on my side of the contract.

Maybe that's more the picture of peace we ought to be after than some nicely paved detour around the mess and dirt of conflict. Rather than passive, unerringly polite people, perhaps the children of God ought to be practicing a dogged refusal to budge from an insistence on peace—an insistence that snarls and clamps down and will not let go of the goal.

Perhaps even in the midst of wildly differing views on *if* and *when* and *where* and *how* wars ought to be fought, we could begin with the small things: landmines, for example. Small things that kill as many as twenty thousand people a year, 80 percent of those killed, civilians. Not only are children most likely to reach for the peculiar, toy-looking devices, but children, being smaller, are most likely to die from their explosion.

I watch my own children's legs even now racing across their backyard: One pair of those legs are as long as my own, and fleet with a soccer ball at her toes; one pair is scrambling up a white pine; and the littlest pair is covered in sand and stiff like a gull's from her fluttering body, legs that would be only two swipes of a pencil if I were to draw her.

Perhaps peace, then, is paying attention to my children and the lives of other children—being fiercely protective of both.

T.S. Eliot quotes Julian of Norwich when he writes, "'And all shall be well and all manner of thing shall be well,'" followed by his added note: "'When the tongues of flame are in-folded / Into the crowned knot of fire / And the fire and the rose are one.'" Again, we're reminded, the

God we follow is familiar with sorrows, acquainted with grief, and knows the beauty that is born of an ultimate peace

The process is not one we could predict. Jesus says, *I did not come to bring peace to the earth, but a sword.* Which would seem to contradict everything else that he said of himself, and that the prophets proclaimed about him. Is he not the Prince of Peace?

So what happened to the lion and the lamb?

A sword, Jesus says, perhaps because peace is not something you achieve lying down, because peace does not always arrive at our doorstep while we're reading home-improvement magazines and noshing on bagels. Perhaps Jesus is saying that *his* kind of peace must be pursued, must be chased after and hunted with unflagging aggression— the violence of love, the cutting keenness of purpose.

Jesus' peace has little to do with my kind of peace, which is the absence of conflict to upset the flow of my day.

Perhaps Jesus' peacemaking involves interruption and distraction and hurry—nothing particularly peaceful on the face of it—yet it makes a difference in how the world runs. Peace, then, would not always be quiet. Or still.

Perhaps peace can be both a supreme contentment of spirit *and* a towering, outspoken courage I don't naturally come by. But we have access to courage enough to back the ultimate aggression: the march forward of peace.

Not peace, Jesus said, *but a sword.*

Which will be, in due time, beaten back into pruning hooks and plowshares.

I remember the man at the march, his finger wagging, his voice with its menacing edge. I try to picture plowshares that my enemy and I could, perhaps, learn to hold in the row together, his weight behind one handle and mine on the other, together tilling a field.

Side by side, perhaps, one day as friends.

So long as he quits harassing my daughter.

Or maybe never as friends. Maybe always eying each other at the other side of the harness with dislike, suspicion, but still bound by our common respect for our common work.

Because despite all natural inclinations toward vengeance or toward calm at all costs, the Prince of Peace calls us to this: kindling concern for each other's children, gathering care for each other's good, persistently stoking the flames of the fires of peace, and someday enfolding this fire into the rose.

7
Blessedness

To say that God chose to walk on earth amongst the poor and lowly makes for quaint nativity scenes and moving lyrics of hymns, but what if Jesus still chooses to move among those who might just be the kind of folks from whom we'd most like to distance ourselves?

"He's such a redneck," my big brother David muttered to me. To illustrate his point, David recounted some latest antic of this, one of his fellow middle school football players who came from the "backside" of the mountain where we grew up in East Tennessee.

I nodded, the little sister eager to show I got the point. "Yeah, what a redn—."

"We don't," our mother scolded from the other side of the kitchen, "call people rednecks."

But David repeated his teammate's behavior, uncouth and crude. And very like every other middle school boy, our mother may have been thinking.

Backing big brother up, I snickered.

"Yes," our mother persisted, rummaging for the splatter screen as the fried chicken began to spit, "but we *don't* call people rednecks."

My brother and I exchanged glances that said simply, *why the heck not when that's what someone just is?*

What are labels for if not to designate and divide and point out? Our mother's linen closet bore labels every eight inches on every shelf: *fitted single bedsheets, baby blankets, flat queen bedsheets, pillowcases.* Labels were how you knew what you were dealing with, weren't they? A fitted twin sheet or a first-cabin redneck. It was helpful to know.

Over the years, my brother grew a compassionate heart and confined most of his middle-school-boy comments to the privacy of his own hearth. He began a professional life in Washington, D.C., where he polished a politically correct vocabulary that mostly excludes the term *redneck.*

I, on the other hand, began my professional life in Boston, where I quickly learned that I was a redneck of the first order.

I first understood I was an illiterate, inbred, backwater hick when I moved to New England. True, I started life in the North with a Southern accent, an eighties blonde perm, a Tennessee license plate, and a deep discomfort in and around shoes. It is also true that my favorite pair of shorts were cutoffs. If you had very poor eyesight, I resembled a less-winsome Ellie May Clampett.

But it was news to me that Southerners couldn't read.

A good friend of mine who'd spent his adult life in New England once referred, from the pulpit of our Cambridge, Massachusetts, church, to a woman who'd once challenged his faith. "But," he described her to us congregants, "she'd grown up poor in the South, so of course she couldn't read."

"So OF COURSE she couldn't . . . ?"

No one but the handful of Southerners in our church even noticed the statement as anything but eternal truth.

I became accustomed to having people ask, after they'd gotten an earful of accent, "where *in the South* are you from" with a patronizing smile.

Time for a one-woman re-education campaign. I tried subtly telling stories in public settings that involved the home of my childhood best friend, whose parents quoted Shakespeare as part of everyday conversation and whose bedside tables were stacked with all the best books and the latest issue of *The New Yorker*. An African mask hung over one door and a stone Celtic cross by the porch—souvenirs from their latest travels.

Now, just between you and me, I knew the Other South too. Any number of the girls from the "backside" of our mountain began disappearing in junior high and never reappeared, the truancy officers apparently lost to this day in a tangle of mountain laurel, moonshine stills, and shotgun muzzles.

But I mentioned none of this to my new northern friends and co-workers. I did not describe how the cool boys in my high school dipped Skoal, or how my family and I had once been stopped at a KKK roadblock. The boys in bedsheets had clutched fast food chicken buckets in which they collected "donations," encouraged by the rifles they nosed in the driver's side window—an opportunity that our car's driver, my father, firmly declined.

No need to bring all that up.

Instead, I got defensive, painting the South as a place of intellectual vitality and current—okay, not past—racial harmony, and pointing out that Boston's South End wasn't exactly known for putting out the welcome mat for African Americans. We'd all seen sixties newsreels of their attacking school buses, right?

I tried to instruct my northern friends in the differences between the South and the Redneck South (since my mother was a safe thousand miles out of earshot)—between the kinds of Southerners who listened to opera, as my mother's family had, and the kinds of Southerners who listened to "Dixie" play on the horns of pickups.

But my friends and colleagues in New England weren't falling for it. The South was one South to them, I discovered: a horrific stew of Beverly Hillbillies and Bull O'Connor.

I tried standing them down.

I made little headway.

In a graduate seminar on southern literature, we read Flannery O'Connor and then watched a video production of her marvelous short story "The Displaced Person."

"Well," our professor, a highly refined woman from the south of India, asked after the viewing. "What did you think?"

I listened for others' scintillating commentary on what O'Connor does theologically, the connections she makes with the refugee family, despised and rejected and abused— the father of the family, an intriguing Christ figure, eventually killed.

A talented poet in our New England classroom was the first to speak. "The casting, I think we'd have to agree, was tremendous in portraying the South: you know, overweight, anemic, inbred. . . ."

The seminar's eyes shifted toward me before the poet finished her sentence.

I'd tried defending myself by sorting people into discernible types: the standard *Us* and *Them*.

But nobody bought it.

Last Monday night, my family and I cooked dinner at a local shelter for homeless families, Safe Haven. We like to think of ourselves as regulars now, becoming familiar with the large industrial kitchen, where its plastic wrap and potholders hide. It's a nice facility. In fact, the first time we showed up on Third Street and my kids got a good look at the vaulted ceiling of the central room, the high-definition TV, and the bunk beds, something my son had been asking annually for from an apparently bankrupt Santa, they turned to us with a *look* in their eyes: *HelLO. What are we doing here helping these people when* they're *the ones with the home theater options?*

On one recent visit, three siblings from the shelter joined us in the kitchen. The three children offered politely to help, though we could barely make out the offer through a swamp of slurred, soggy vowels, and deep-woods accent.

The oldest girl, just a year younger than my middle school daughter, hedged when we asked her what grade she was in. The question clearly upset her.

"Well, see, everybody asks that, and. . . . " Her eyes filled with tears. "And I never know what to tell them. It ain't my fault is what I tell them. Ain't my fault I can't read."

The girl went on from there, her two younger brothers, both of them also unable to read, chiming in with commentary on the schools they'd attended, the grades they had failed thus far.

Their mother appeared at dinner. She was probably younger than I am by a good decade, and with several lifetimes of pain on her face.

On the way home in the car, my kids considered what it would be like to have changed schools every few months, or to have no place of their own, a quiet table or spot to spread out their books, no second parent to help with somebody's phonics while the other fixes the dinner. And no authorities to know somebody's skipped school again

and again, because the place of residence is listed nowhere
a truancy officer could find it on file, because you have no
permanent home.

"What about," my seven-year-old son wanted to know,
"that lady who was like us?"

I was guessing I knew who he meant, but I asked anyway.
"You mean Metra?"

"Yeah. The lady with the nice, flipped-up hair, and the
smile."

I nodded. Of course that's who he'd seen as Like Us. Not
the Caucasian kids, who were two of my three kids' same
race and all of their same ages, but the African American
young woman who'd helped us haul out the drinks.

Metra had crossed the room when we'd arrived and
introduced herself. Friendly, well-spoken, and poised—
and with a killer haircut—she'd offered her assistance and
chatted as we'd rummaged for pans. We spoke of where she
was in graduate school, and what she was planning next.

Like Us, my son had determined.

Like Us: perhaps because her teeth were so unerringly
straight—better aligned than any of those in our family. Or
her clothes, though jeans like everyone else's that night, had
fades and frays that looked more Old Navy than actually
old. Or because her self-assurance said volumes about her
knowing she was anyone's equal. Or because nothing about
her looked beaten or battered or used up and trampled.
Nothing about her looked the least bit defensive, waiting
to strike back at ugly assumptions about who she was.
Because any assumptions about Metra would have to

include that she has more money and education—and a better hairstylist—than you.

My seven-year-old son had somehow already mastered his mother's fine art of sorting, not by race—that's only for rednecks, you know—but by education, by social standing, by how a person carries herself.

Surely more than any story of a god's contact with mortals, the appearance of Jesus on earth messed with categories of Us and Not Us. This God chooses a young woman not for urbane sophistication or education or a great haircut, but for her spirit of servanthood, her good heart, and her pluck. Jesus' mother, Mary, meek and mild, wasn't even part of the respectable middle class. And at least in the eyes of some of the neighbors, she wasn't even a Good Girl, having borne that child far too early, even though Joseph tried to make an honest woman of her.

There's the donkey ride to Bethlehem and nobody's giving this couple the time of day, much less a room, and the barn that serves as maternity ward. The stuff of Not Us.

The ceramic, hand-painted nativity scene displayed in our dining room is the romantic Hallmark card scene we all treasure: No manure clings to the tails of the sheep; the camels are not clumsy, not nosing out the cattle for a drink in the trough. None of the shepherds are missing teeth or reek of strong drink. The Wise Men, handsome and pleasantly racially diverse, having arrived a couple of years ahead of schedule in order to be included in the ceramic casting. Slender, well-manicured ceramic Mary has lost all her pregnancy flab while Joseph appears well rested and calm, as if he's been helping deliver babies who are not his and laying them in cattle troughs every day for the past year.

I love this nativity scene.

I'm uneasy going down this road, but here's the thing: I'm guessing the shepherds in that culture were several social rungs below rednecks—if you'll forgive my using the word.

From what biblical scholars tell us, shepherds as a social group didn't *choose* watching sheep as a professional calling so much as they were already outcasts, already on the run from the majority culture, already seen as uneducated, crude, tending toward the illiterate, poorly groomed, and more than a little murky on personal hygiene. *Abiding in the field* was where the townspeople preferred them. Shepherds were people who couldn't afford the mobile homes of their richer kin, and so slept outdoors with the sheep.

These were a people who were not well traveled, well read, or well bred—at best they were repulsive, boorish—and boring. In his poem "At the Manger," one of W.H. Auden's shepherds comments that they have "walked a thousand miles yet only worn / The grass between our work and home away."

Now at that most pigeonholing of ages, my middle-school-aged child just yesterday startled me.

"He's *such* a loser," she concluded her story to her younger brother, who, as always, chortled, nodding so hard he nearly choked on his grapes.

"Yeah," he was quick to agree. "What a los—"

"We *don't*," I called from the kitchen, "call people losers." A room away, I couldn't see their two faces, but still knew their glances that said how Mom didn't get how some people just *were*.

"*Got that?*" I called in to the smirks.

"Yes, ma'am," they quickly called back.

Just moments before, I labeled my daughter's age group, middle school, as that most pigeonholing of ages. But we adults function much the same way, don't we? Is it that we never quite outgrow our childhood tendencies to divide the rocks we've collected into igneous and metamorphosis, and the people we know into winners and losers, into nice people *without* rusted-out cars in front yards, and, oh, rednecks? Or do children learn from adults about the thrills of categorization: the rich and the poor, the majority and minority race, the educated and uneducated, who would be, of course, no one in our own homes?

Jesus, the writer of the Gospel of Luke is so anxious to explain, comes into this story of a minority-culture, working-class, surely illiterate Nobody girl. An angel announces she is highly favored by God.

Then a whole sky of angels show up to a group of loser-rednecks in the fields, just them and their stench and their pasts and their uselessness and their flasks. Then here comes a sky full of razzle-dazzle and wings, and the heavens are blazing and ringing with song, and the shepherds choke on their wads of tobacco and trip over their bottles of Night Train and shake in a huddle together. And then they're all sobbing, just like you and I would, because they're so scared, despite the command to *fear not*, and they're amazed.

Surely that means things are never the same. Because the God who tossed the planets in place has announced that for those made in the divine image, this pigeonholing and categorizing and labeling will no longer work. That the social order as we once knew it has been trumped.

"Blessed," says Luke, quoting the baby born in the cow barn who grows up to be Jesus, "blessed are the poor." Blessed.

Blessed are those of you out there who don't know how you'll buy groceries this month.

Blessed are you who scrape together the dollars and dimes to take a feverish child to the doctor.

Blessed are you because true blessings have nothing to do with money, and money can trip you up badly, like that poor, rich young ruler, in the path to finding true riches.

Blessed are you whose education was lacking because you were homeless.

Blessed are you who run bases with a pronounced limp, for you will teach others about real power and strength.

Blessed are you when your appearance has caused wrong assumptions.

Blessed: when because of your skin color and the fact that today you wore jeans, the hospital patients assumed you were the maid instead of the surgeon.

Blessed: when the chair of the board assumes that because you're a woman, you couldn't do the job.

Blessed.

Because: God sees. God cringes. God weeps. God balls up a fist with you.

God lowers the gavel.

Because God has shown up in flesh in a way that announced with one heck of a public address system that if there's any partisanship in the heavenly realm, it's on the side of the crowd who is misunderstood, who never yet got their fair share. But will.

The truth is, this good news is bad news—is appalling news, really—if we're still at the table dividing our rocks and our stamps and the people we know. If we've got ourselves in the box with the gemstones, the wealthy and the winners. The Arrived. The Accepted. The In.

The news is horrific if we've got ourselves at the top of the food chain, and someone just upended the chain.

The gospel becomes good news only if we've somehow wised up and lumped ourselves alongside the losers and strugglers, alongside those who've somehow, in some way, royally messed up, been pushed out, or once pushed others out and are now grieving about it. If we know the inside story about who we are, about all we're lacking, despite all that the outside world thinks we've achieved.

Good news: to all of us rednecks and losers and mess-ups, with the lingering stench of old sins, the done and not done.

Good news to those left out of the loop. Good news to those who were forgotten.

There are in the same country with us shepherds. Fear not.

For unto you is born a whole different way of thinking, of seeing how you're doing in life.

Unto you is begun a hierarchy turned on its head. A mixing up of the segregations. A muddling up of the social classes.

A messy, glass-all-over-the-road kind of collision of Us and Them. And healing will follow.

Not exactly what we were hoping?

Maybe that's why it's a command: *Fear not!*

For unto us, us misunderstood, us passed over, us rednecks and losers who've discovered we bear the image of God, us the breath-knocked-out-of-us grateful who fall with our faces to the frozen scraggly field, unto *us* is born this day, in the city of David, a Savior, which is Christ the Lord.

8
Worship

A group of us had read the fifty-eighth chapter of the prophet Isaiah, and we had agreed upon how the celebration of Sabbath, the practice of worship, should happen: not by fancy displays and in-your-face fasting, but in feeding the hungry, and clothing the naked, and not turning away from our own flesh and blood, which is all humankind.

We knew just what true worship looked like. Basically, it looked like us.

These friends and I brainstormed what we could do in grateful response to God's goodness: how we could worship inside but also outside a church sanctuary. We'd noticed how pointedly Jesus tells the story of the rich man and Lazarus. How in life the rich man manages to keep his Italian leather unscuffed by stepping clear over beggars at his doorstep. But in death, this same man finds himself unable to cross into heaven. We'd observed how worship among the people hanging out with Jesus happened not in the places set out for worship—the temples, the Holy of Holies—but as they watch him in action. From shore to where his friends are fishing in the middle of a big lake, Jesus walks on the water to them. Despite the lack of firm footing. Despite a big wind and waves. Seeing Jesus coming, impetuous Peter leaps out of the boat, only to sink. And though Jesus rescues Peter, gets the two of them safely into the boat, everyone watching is shaken. And Peter is soaked. The disciples drop to the deck in what Matthew calls worship, and I'm guessing it's safe to read into the worship some terror there, too.

New Testament worship often goes hand in hand with a good shaking up, or gorgeous acts of absurd faith and near felonies, like guys lowering a sick friend down through a hole vandalized into a roof because Jesus is surrounded by crowds underneath. Pleading for the healing of her daughter, a desperate Canaanite woman collapses in a posture of worship, right down to the kneecaps she drops to the dirt at both the unpredictable power and the always compassion of this Jesus.

In fact, when Jesus does show up in official houses of worship, he's more likely to be wielding a whip at the money tables of those abusing the poor than he is to be carting a hymnbook.

My friends and I had studied all this, and we'd served in soup kitchens populated primarily by homeless men, and helped break up fights there. We'd discovered, by experience and by research, that safe, comfortable venues for homeless and low-income women and families were lacking in Cambridge.

My only leadership qualification in this area being a slight deafness to all the explanations of what *couldn't* be done, I became the director, soon joined by my friend and co-worker Kitty. *You have no funding, no space, no staff,* people insisted in that slow, too-patient tone reserved for the not-very-bright. But Kitty shook hands with hostile neighbors, invited them in, and soon they were hauling boxes down the steep stairwells of our church.

We collected cash and canned food and khakis and down coats from our congregation, and we tunneled out a portion of the church basement that had been used in the nineteenth century for trash and coal dust disposal. Interestingly, no one objected to our taking this space. So we planned and we gathered canned goods and clothes, and we harassed local merchants into donating free stuff. We advertised all over town that a new food pantry was opening, targeted specifically for women and families, and that we would be a reliable source for emergency child-specific needs. We prayed and we spoke of that day when the grateful masses would gather.

Being a church with a strange demographic of primarily university students and singles and young married couples, we'd been given mountains of nearly new clothes from the

Gap and Ann Taylor—but no infant clothes. We had only the diapers we'd bought at full price from the grocery, and a grand total of two sets of baby clothes. Gorgeous and warm and recently hand-knitted, but numbering only two.

We did have, though, towers of jarred baby food and canned goods and bread and day-old bakery pastries. We could feed half the city, at least for one meal.

We told and re-told each other how Jesus multiplied loaves and fishes, a miracle that led to surprise and confusion and wonder—and worship that day, and still does.

The big moment arrived to open for the very first time: a historic day.

We marched to the imposing, heavy-arched doors, built to match our church's imposing, fortress-like architecture, as if built to keep those riff-raff peasants at bay.

Here to save our city's suffering poor from further socio-economic oppression at precisely ten o'clock on a frigid, gray November day, we flung open the doors. To a grand total of . . . no one waiting there.

No one.

We checked our watches. It was indeed ten o'clock. We strained our necks for the long, snaking line that should be there.

Not one single soul.

This was followed by wonder. Not the worshipful wonder we'd planned, but rather a what-the-heck wonder: where had the hungry, clambering masses gone?

Then, at the corner, a woman pushing a baby carriage appeared. Teri helped haul the stroller up the church's steep steps. Her husband, Rick, scrambled to join her.

They warmly welcomed the woman, even as they bent both their heads down toward the stroller, cooing softly, "Ohhhhh," for the baby they couldn't wait to see.

Followed by another "Ohhhhh," this one thinner and weaker, a kind of tinny, time-staller sound, Teri and Rick's backs bent down toward the carriage, their faces frozen.

Then came a last "Ohhhhh!" their heads lifted now, facing me with alarm.

I joined them at the stroller, holding my hand out to the woman. She introduced us to her baby, whose name, she informed us, was Garfield.

Which I could see for myself.

Because it was, in fact, a stuffed orange cat.

The baby was Garfield. Our first customer of this grand opening day. This holy moment of justice, mercy, and worship.

Over the course of the next hour, we offered the woman every kind of food we had in the pantry—and we had hundreds of kinds. *Tuna? Gefilte fish? Peanut butter? Won't you sit down—you and Garfield—and rest? Cream cheese croissant while you—the two of you—sit?*

But first off, the woman insisted, she needed warm clothes for Garfield.

Teri and Rick, two of the most compassionate souls ever to hand out a can of green beans, looked at me. The three of us looked at the two, only two, hand-knitted baby outfits we had on the shelf.

"May I have both?" the woman wanted to know.

Which was when my compassionate co-workers completely bailed out and left it to me.

I thought of the long, snaking lines of single mothers with shivering infants who had probably already queued up by now outside the door. I thought of the temperature, below freezing, and of the long New England winter before us.

I laid a hand that was meant to look tenderly sympathetic on the woman's shoulder. The truth was, I was embarrassed and not at all happy. Here we were, prepared and well-stocked to bring hope to the hopeless, and thanks to the recent deinstitutionalization of so many mentally ill patients, and thanks to this woman's showing up *now* of all times, we were dealing with not cold, hungry women and families, but a stuffed cat. And only a stuffed cat.

I explained in the most reasonable of tones that since other *real* babies would be needing warm clothing this winter, perhaps she could take only one outfit for her . . . um . . . Garfield.

The next thing I knew she was leaving—without a single can or loaf for herself. And she informed me she'd have her lover hunt me down with her lover's knife. Kept sharpened, she added.

So *this* was true worship?

Because, with all due respect to the prophets and Jesus, I felt in no mood for adoring the Alpha and the Omega, Maker of Heaven and Earth. I felt slimy, angry, annoyed, and in need of a personal bodyguard.

Our faithful experiment with worship-through-loaves-
and-fishes seemed to have rotted right there in the
tunneled-out basement.

Aware that we had no funding to speak of, and that our
opening day had been reason enough to close the world's
finest food pantry for homeless families altogether, I walked
home in despair.

I was not meditating on the word *worship*. Or how it
derives from *worth*ship, the *th* only being dropped in the
fourteenth century. Or how it's because God is worthy of
our adoration that we worship, and because those made in
the image of God are worthy of our respect that we serve.
And the *-ship* of the worth/worship: the understanding
that this is something we're on board with together. This
same ideal caused the architects of medieval cathedrals to
build sanctuaries in the long shape of a ship—even naming
these main sections "naves," from the Latin, *navis*, for ship:
all of us journeying together, with God, to God.

All this I'd managed to forget in one single morning—
just me, journeying alone. Sulking.

I drowned my sorrows in perm solution.

Now a $6.98 home perm kit may not be the best route
to spiritual recovery to begin with. Nor is it necessarily the
best route to an "extreme makeover." Given its chemical
harshness, it is absolutely imperative, the directions stress, to
wash out the solution within the allotted time. Otherwise,
the hair will burn, and the manufacturer cannot be held

responsible for the ensuing fuzz.

Vile-smelling solution all over my head, a far cry from the incense of worship I'd intended to offer that day, it occurred to me I might turn to Scripture for comfort, and return to a spirit of worship.

Instead, I found a newspaper, and then the phone rang. Clearly, I should not get it, since the solution was ready to be washed out.

But the voice on the answering machine was our church treasurer, Laura, who'd championed the food pantry from the beginning.

I could hear her smiling on the other end of the line.

I picked up, explaining I had to get to the shower in thirty seconds, or there'd be fuzz to pay. "The pantry's grand opening," I then volunteered, "was a disaster this morning."

"I know. But that's not why I called. Are you sitting down?"

I wasn't. Too busy sulking.

"I have a check here," she went on, "from an anonymous donor. It's designated for the running of the food pantry." She told me the amount.

I sat down.

And there was another check too, a grant I'd applied for that we'd assumed we hadn't gotten.

One of us stunned, then both of us giddy, Laura and I both talked at the same time, my trying to wheedle the donor's identity from her, her refusing to budge, both of us dreaming of the food pantry's future.

A good forty minutes later when I set the phone down, I smelled something peculiar, something spoiled and charred and swamplike. . . .

Fried hair.

It took four years for fifteen inches of fuzz to grow out, but it served as a vivid reminder.

As it turns out, one can worship quite well with a headful of blonde wires.

The food pantry began to grow, and then thrive. Over the years, God brought snaking lines of clients from all over the world, often with no coats or jobs or food for our long New England winters, and bread, mountains of baked goods from a local bakery, and money, checks flowing in from the strangest of places, often unsought, and towering stacks of food and racks of clothing, often designer labels never worn, and hundreds of volunteers.

Nearly twenty years later and now under different and no doubt more able leadership, the Cambridgeport Clothes Closet/Food Pantry lives on, now called Harvest. Despite our pathetic beginnings and shortcomings and stumbles, we clung to the hope that God could somehow work even low-level, B-movie wonders from what meager offerings we showed up with.

Here was God's power, God's abundance—far more than we could ask or imagine.

Still, it was often a hard road to worship, with casualties along the way: my hair, for example. Our in-the-trenches experience also destroyed a too-easy innocence, our ability to spout slick, one-size-fits-all answers to urban poverty. As we watched the crowds come, we wondered each week if the food and the money and the clothes and the free labor would keep coming too. We found ourselves frequently fearful, frequently fretful, but always amazed.

Which leads well to worship—of a not terribly comfortable sort.

In a more sweetly immediate sense, here's what *feels* more like worship to me.

Just south of Nashville, where I currently live, the hills are alive and well-watered by the sound and economic trickle-down of music. The music *industry*, that is.

When dining out in New York, chances are your waiter is an aspiring actor, and in Boston, the person who serves up your pizza is more than likely an angst-ridden wanna-be writer. Here in Nashville, the young lady who ladles out your lasagna is either a songwriter, strings player, or singer. Music City is flooded with musical talent, so deluged in fact that any given nightclub, hotel bar, tavern, and church, no matter how seedy or mind-altered its listeners, can play host any given week to unbelievable, platinum talent.

In Nashville, in churches, we call some of these performances worship.

When last I checked, the kind of person who both enjoys and benefits from something and then condemns it is called a hypocrite, so let me be clear. I admire and celebrate an enormously talented person's giving her best straight to God. And I appreciate getting to be there to watch, especially when there's no cover charge—not counting the tithe.

But I'm aware that there are many weeks when my own heart defines worship according to the crescendo of the live orchestra, or the name recognition of the faces upfront. In some local churches, the pianist may also play keyboard for Disney. A random guest soloist might have just cut a recent top ten in country western or gospel or hip hop. Worship services here often bring me to tears for their artistic beauty, for the sheer power, the towering risk of the trumpets' high notes, the white water rush of the harp, the lyrics that assure me of God's mercy toward me, against all the odds and the neighbors' predictions.

So I quite cheerfully show up for worship services here, not just dragging myself as a noble example for the impressionable small people who live in my house. Worship here is often full of wonder and awe, and of professional polish.

And as a spectator, I'm grateful.

Except that sometimes, even in the midst of feeling soul-fuzzy and worshipful, as the trumpets reach their trill, high and clear, I wonder if this is more about my feeling good than it is about God. I don't doubt the trumpeters' gift to God in playing. But some days, I do doubt how much of a gift I'm giving God by showing up to listen, and going away with my spiritual carbonation re-bubbled.

Because, all Garfields aside, there's no getting around this whole thing of worship as defined by the prophets and the behavior of Jesus and the gospel writers depicting just what he was about. Their definitions, quite frankly, I find disturbing.

As best I can make out, the assumption seems to be that the first step in preparing our insides for true worship of God is to start by examining the external, supposedly non-spiritual parts of our lives. How we treat workers and widows and orphans, how we handle our jobs and our banking, our dealings with those who have less influence than we do. Real worship in Jesus' life had more to do with the hungry and hurting, about mercy and compassion, than about traditional worship in a particular setting on a particular day. In the first recorded time he reads from the Sacred Scriptures in the synagogue, Jesus chooses Isaiah: I've come

to proclaim good news to the poor,
He has sent me to bind up the brokenhearted
to proclaim freedom for the captives. . . .

Then he lets his listeners know that the Messiah the passage describes has arrived. In the flesh.

With this, Jesus slaps the would-be worshipers right out of their half-listening slumps. Suddenly, they're paying attention. And they're enraged.

Worship is sacrifice, Isaiah argues, not of calves on the altar, but of who we are, and how we deal with the world. Jesus takes up and lives out the theme.

In his letter to Rome, the apostle Paul picks up the baton

here when he urges the faithful "in view of God's mercy, to offer your bodies as a living sacrifice, holy and pleasing to God—this is true worship."

Like Isaiah and Jesus, this sounds good on the face of it—just and admirable. Good at a safe distance, that is.

I have my own clear and bracing lesson on becoming a living sacrifice for a purpose outside myself. And in the interest of full disclosure, let me just say that I did not handle it with grace or style. Or dignity.

One reads of women who *glow* when they are pregnant, who will tell you straight-faced they have never felt better in their lives. I was one of the *other* kind, whose waistline reaches such monumental proportions that small children, large dogs, and the unwary in wheelchairs are in danger of being smacked in the face. I was the kind whose hair goes limp and whose skin goes sallow and veins go varicose, the kind whose maternity wardrobe comes from the makers of Coleman tents. The creature to whom I'd apparently turned over full control of my mind, schedule, and physical person had decided to conduct extensive renovations inside my body, on which the creature hammered away all night every night.

Still living in Boston, I was thirty when I became pregnant with my first child. "So," I said to my doctor, "my body *will* spring back to its original shape. Right?" The doctor was busily writing notes to herself. But I still wanted my reassurance. "I mean, after . . . all this. I'll fit in my old jeans again." She wasn't answering quickly enough. "Right?"

She sized me up unsympathetically over her clipboard. "If you were sixteen, maybe." She rose to leave.

"But . . . wait . . . what about my internal organs? I can hardly breathe, and I have weeks to go. Where exactly do my internal organs . . . go?"

"Wherever," she snapped, "they have to. They'll squeeze up behind your ribs, behind, around—under your chin, if they have to. The *point*," she turned on her heel to be sure I was paying attention, "is to make room for the baby."

"Yes, I mean, *of course,* but . . . that is, I would like to think that at some point by the end of all this I could still, you know, like . . . breathe."

She was already at the door, and only tossed this back over her shoulder: "You breathe when you can . . . *if* you can. *Your* job is just to make room."

Living sacrifice equals true worship, we learn, which means first making room. And sacrifice involves what we have, what we hold, what we'd like to hoard. It's inside and out. The whole shebang. Available for additions and renovations. Prepared for total gutting, if necessary. Braced to be used as a center for spiritual birth, our own and others'.

All that we are, turned over to God, for God's use. Our job, to make room.

Which brings us back, whether I like it or not, to Garfield.

Sometime after it was clear I would probably not be jumped in a dark alley by a stuffed cat's mother's lover wielding a knife, I called my sister-in-law. Beth is a chaplain who once worked at a psychiatric hospital. I reported the scene of our pantry's opening day to Beth, omitting the ending.

"It's really important," Beth told me, "in dealing with this kind of thing not to contradict directly the person's delusion."

"You mean, like, if I were to have said something along the lines of 'Let's leave these warm winter clothes for a *real* baby?'"

"Exactly. You would never want to say something like that."

"Right," I said. "Good to know."

"So what did you say to . . . ?"

"Golly, would you look at the time! Listen, thanks for the help. Oh, and . . . just for the record, any idea what causes this kind of delusion?"

"Sometimes these things are rooted in some kind of trauma, and the person's mind gets stuck there."

"Like . . . ?"

"Like, for example, maybe this woman lost a baby in a tragic accident. So she's transferred that pain and that loss to. . . ."

I suddenly felt sick at my stomach. "To her baby. Her . . . Garfield."

"So," Beth asked again, "how *did* you handle the situation?"

I'd like to tell you that I saw the woman again, that government funding had restored her access to psychiatric meds, that our congregation enveloped her in restoring compassion, that I had the chance to apologize for being annoyed by her presence, for my not understanding . . . anything.

The truth is, I never saw her again, except in a couple of dreams—nightmares. My husband and I had researched the history of our quirky old farmhouse, built in 1811, and had discovered that the first owners, parents of seven, suffered their youngest child's death in a fire in the house. Which explained the charred wallpaper on the bottoms of basement floorboards some economizing soul had torn out after the fire and reused.

So in the nightmares I had of the Cambridgeport Food Pantry's first guest, I pictured her frantically fighting flames to get to her baby. I'd wake, shaken, sometimes in tears, and years later, feeling frantically for the crib at the foot of my bed.

In any case, I can say categorically I did absolutely no good for this woman at all. Except that sometimes I prayed for her, and still do.

And I can tell you that the Cambridgeport pantry that opened to so inauspicious a start did indeed soon see lines that snaked down the street before the doors opened each Saturday morning. That these families taught me, taught all of us a good deal about the nature of God. That hoards of Wellesley and Harvard and Tufts and MIT students who spoke an array of languages showed up over the weeks and the years to help us translate, and do intake, and pack grocery bags, and sort clothing donations, including baby outfits. I can tell you that more able hands than mine eventually took charge of the ministry, and expanded and bettered it.

I can tell you that, having cradled three babies now of my own, I find it perfectly sane that the loss of a child might freeze one's mind in one single place. That the most reasonable thing in the world would be never, never completely moving past that wasteland of loss.

I can tell you now that I am still learning about worship. About sacrifice and compassion. About the ways we offer ourselves up to God. And the ways we do not.

The writer Annie Dillard suggests that if we took this idea of approaching holiness more seriously instead of with our pathetically low expectations, we'd all wear crash helmets to worship.

Or maybe, I'd add, pith helmets, as miners do, for danger and going down deep. Pith helmets with a light on the front, for when we can't quite make out what we're seeing.

Like our own flesh and blood. Disturbing as that may be.

To worship is to prepare for the uncomfortable. For God's showing up, often not when and how we expect.

To dig out, make room for change and birth and re-birth.

Worship with cymbals and the clatter of clothes-closet racks. In stained-glass cathedrals and dank basements.

Everything we have and we are on the altar, laid down with awe for a God whose ways are not our ways but whose face is all around us.

With gratitude for a God whose love flows like the deep end of the ocean, and whose power is bound to catch us up short, knock us clear to our knees.

This is true worship.

9
Forgiveness

On my husband's Italian side of the family—*la Familia,* shouted, with hands above the head—are stories, colorful and outlandish and founded at least partly on fact, of Mafia involvement.

I relish these stories, partly because they're well told, and partly out of envy. I come from a long line of British Isles folk: tweedy, bookish, armed-with-umbrella people who, once wronged, may stew and let wounds fester. But rarely do we indulge in a good fit of vengeance.

"Leave the gun, take the cannoli," goes that great line from *The Godfather,* just after a killing to settle a score.

In my family culture, frustrated rage may not slam a door (bad form) or avoid speaking to someone (bad manners). One can vent one's ire only in slugging one's pillow in the dark of the night.

As I implied in an earlier chapter, hoping no one would notice, I have been a gold-medal grudge-holder, training long hours in season and out.

Except I fear that my best grudge-holding days are behind me.

It's one casualty of growing older, I suppose, if you've grown older as I have, by making a boatload of mistakes. This form of learning limits the store of self-righteousness one can keep a good hold on.

Most days I don't like just how this whole thing of forgiveness works, really.

It's nothing like our judicial system, where the punishment fits the crime. And it's nothing like my fantasy world of soft-spoken female Mafioso, where the punishment far exceeds the crime.

Forgiveness as defined by the gospel has nothing to do with fairness.

If we're honest, most of us measure whether someone deserves to be forgiven on a Willy Wonka–like scale: All Bad Eggs remain unabsolved, and are promptly sent down the pipes. Good Eggs, on the other hand, could hang out with us.

We often turn Jesus into a scowling, white-bearded judge, with, as poet Billy Collins depicts it, "a golden ladder on one side, a coal chute on the other."

It's how most of us think most of the time.

Take my dear son, for example. Justin may not be much of a theological scholar, but he has really nice hair. Which, it turns out, will get you a long way in life. And he's a generally good judge of character. One winter evening just a few nights ago, my husband was recounting the good deeds of an older gentleman, Wiley Scott, who spends holidays volunteering at the local Nashville Toy Store, where low-income families use vouchers to "purchase" Christmas gifts for their children. He uses up all his vacation days for this.

Justin listened, wide-eyed, then: "Whoa. He is *sooooo* going to heaven."

Now *this* calculation by Justin makes lots of sense.

Not to Jesus, though.

Jesus might pat our saintly friend Wiley Scott on the back with a hearty, "Well done, my good man." But he also turns, in his own final hour, to the thief on the cross, a guy who surely stole more than one loaf of bread—a career criminal. But when the thief rips his fellow criminal on the third cross for ridiculing an innocent man, Jesus, and begs to be remembered when Jesus comes into his kingdom, Jesus says, translating loosely, "You are *soooo* coming with me. Today. Right now. Paradise."

It's anything but fair, or predictable, even.

Jesus makes it look easy, this kind of forgiveness of the thief on the cross. He's also asked the Father for forgiveness for the network of folks who put him up on the cross in the first place.

But suppose we put ourselves in the place of the crowd at the foot of the cross—not Jesus' cross, but the thief who's just turned to Jesus. He was trouble all right. He stole your car and totaled it on the way out of town. Stole your laptop and all your data, which cost you your job. He dated your sister, got her pregnant and messed up on drugs. She's still paying the price. And although you can see from the pain on the guy's face that his repentance is real, that maybe he really is sorry and smashed up inside, still, you don't want anybody speaking comfort to him. To you, maybe. And to your family. But not to this guy.

It is simply not *fair*, Jesus' letting this guy tag along into eternal reward.

The longer I live, the more I remain bewildered and befuddled by that.

And also desperately grateful.

Nearly two decades ago, I was fresh from the South, just back from my honeymoon, and a new, wide-eyed resident of Boston. No one, so far as I could tell, met anyone else's eye here. No one in grocery store lines made friendly—or even unfriendly—chatter.

My new husband, Todd, was charging—his one speed in life—out the door, and asked me to come along on an errand. Intending to ride shotgun, I didn't fret over diving into the car without shoes or purse. The car itself, a boxy brown and gold '79 Zephyr with dents and dings in each corner, had been my grandfather's before his oldest son finally insisted on taking his keys. I'd bought the car with the sum total of my life savings. Though it was already a good decade old when we married, my husband and I agreed he'd probably married me for the Zepyhr, as he'd been living carless in Boston, his horizons stretching only to the rail ends of the underground "T."

Now with transportation in Beantown for the first time since his first year at Harvard, Todd was a little boy with Hotwheels, finding the crush of traffic exhilarating.

As he drove, Todd laughed at my bare feet and shook his head. Then, his hand clutching his right eye, he pulled over and motioned for me to trade places with him. "My contact," he said.

"But the traffic . . . I don't know where we. . . ."

Still, I took the wheel.

A little traffic, a little urban impatience, a few horns honked or fingers flipped my direction—how hard could this be?

A former youth minister of mine, Mike Willard, had wisely once taught that often when people vent their anger, they are actually frustrated at something else, not necessarily you, so remember this phrase: *I am not the target.*

For a little distance, these words served me well. All down Massachusetts Avenue, past MIT and toward Harvard. *I am not the target,* I mantraed. Fine down Memorial Drive and Western Avenue: *I am not the target.*

But just as the Western Avenue bridge spans the Charles River to meet Storrow Drive, a snarl of one-way streets converge and a bank of stoplights sway across the street. Not just one light but a whole array, with green arrows and red arrows and yellow flashing lights and red everywhere.

Cyclists swarmed the intersection, arrows flashed, horns bellowed. Cars from three directions barreled toward me. I had no idea which light was mine, or which cyclists were supposed to give way for my car and which I was allowed to run over.

So I did the only reasonable thing: I stopped smack in the middle of the intersection. To think. To be sure I wasn't making an enormous mistake in which light I was heeding.

It seemed a logical choice at the time.

No other motorists seemed to agree.

Fingers flipped all around me. Horns raised their howls together in chorus.

Quite clearly: *I* was *the target.*

My new husband, speechless, was no help at all. *'Til death do us part,* I suspect he was thinking.

It wasn't that I didn't see the police car. It was more that I had no idea what to do, given that now I was surrounded by a tangle of cars and trucks and bikes and people staring at me, and sharing their innermost thoughts.

The lights of the patrol car flashed on. I made my way through the muddle I'd magnificently made, and under the red light that, it turns out, was mine.

The officer, disbelief amounting to awe on his face, marched to my door. He was already shaking his head. Much like my husband—my beloved husband whose fault this whole thing surely was.

Short, slight-built, and with a Caribbean accent, the officer ordered me out of the car.

Todd valiantly began to explain. "You see, officer, she's from. . . ."

The officer pointed to me. "*You,*" he said. "Over here."

He marched me to the back of my car, out of earshot of a husband making excuses for my existence in Boston.

I tenderfooted behind him.

He looked down at my bare feet, dusty and bare, the nails still painted pink from the wedding. He checked my plates, still unchanged since our arrival. Tennessee.

He looked back at me: a Georgia Tech T-shirt, yellow shorts, yellow hair.

Tennessee tags. And no shoes.

"License?" he demanded.

No license.

"Shoes?" he wanted to know.

"Well, now, I do own some, but it's just. . . ."

He shook his head in the direction of the Tennessee plates, then held up his hand.

I stopped talking.

"Did you," he cocked his head at me, "did you ever actually *see* the red light you ran?"

"Which one?" I asked politely, only then realizing that might not help my case. So I added "Sir," which didn't seem to help either. But honestly, there'd been so many lights strung up there, I hadn't seen how anyone could choose only one to obey.

I began speaking again. Often a mistake in my case. As best I recall, I blathered about a wedding only ten days ago in the hills of East Tennessee, about how I came from a town with only one stoplight—or two if you counted the flashing red down by the bank, about how I'd not intended to drive.

The officer held up his hand once again.

Excuses stuck there in my throat.

I was about to be buried, as my father had so often warned, under the jail.

The officer paused, his pad in his hand, his pen poised above the lines. He seemed confounded at where to begin writing me up. Again, he shook his head.

Then he spoke. And he pointed, first at me, then at my car. "Go . . . ," he commanded.

I braced myself for what would follow the "Go": the "to . . ." and what might follow the "to."

Now it was my turn to look down at my feet, my toes dug deep into street grime, down at my Georgia Tech T-shirt, my Tennessee tags.

"*Go*," he said again.

Confused, I began walking backward, still waiting for the ticket, the execution, whatever it was he and I both knew I deserved.

Not taking my eyes off his face, I reversed my way toward the passenger side.

"No," he said then, sternly.

"No?"

"No," he told me and pointed again. "*You* drive."

"Me?" This came out in a squeak.

"You," he nodded. "*Drive.*"

Slowly, timorously, still watching, still shaking, I lifted the driver's side handle.

"*And* . . . ," he shouted over the din of the traffic.

"Yes, sir?"

". . . Welcome to Boston!"

Repeatedly in the accounts of his life, Jesus announces a similar thing to those whose lives have crashed, or are about to: *No, not in the passenger seat. Like it or not, you can't hide from life. What you can do, and what you'd better start now, is quit screwing up . . . and around. Go. And welcome to mercy.*

That day crossing the Charles River from Cambridge to Boston wasn't the worst of my life's mistakes, by fearfully far.

But perhaps one of the more publicly witnessed.

A whole cloud of witnesses, in the form of drivers free with their opinions and their hand motions, watched the policeman swagger toward my car and thought to themselves, *Well, thank God, he'll nail that idiot's hide.* And then they, my fellow motorists, went on their way rejoicing in the comfort of sure justice.

Only justice was never accomplished.

I've since wondered if my police officer's letting me off the legal hook had anything to do with his having once been in my shoes: a newcomer, scared, rattled, unsure.

Because our ability to forgive others takes root and grows only as we understand what we've been forgiven: how much and how improbably and at what cost. Realize just how clearly that burial site under the jail had been ours.

In the gospels, the gang who hangs out with Jesus keeps whining to know, just like I do, how this whole thing of forgiveness could possibly work. And how far do we have to take it? Like children counting out gummies we don't want to share: exactly how many times do we *have* to forgive?

That depends, Jesus responds. *How many times would you like God to forgive you?*

At the tangled junctures of life when I suddenly see what I've done, what damage I've caused or almost have, I stagger about my days overawed, knocked off my feet by forgiveness poured out, with me in the path of the oncoming flood. The grudges I once coddled no longer thrive well—not where I live now: in mercy.

Mercy.

My husband and I recently visited with the Nashville chapter of the NAACP—two washed-out, sun-bleached faces—the dull pale of driftwood—in a sea of more interesting color. Jim Lawson, the architect and the brains behind the Civil Rights Movement, preached, just as he did five decades ago when fire hoses were being aimed at him. He spoke of nonviolence, and forgiveness, and paths forward. I sat there struck with the strange knowledge of having been raised on the mountain that for years hid the assassin of civil rights activist Medgar Evers. And struck again with the knowledge that I descended from a white South that brutalized those whose descendants now sat beside me, who moments ago shook my hand, hugged my neck.

Forgive us, O Lord, our sin. And also our skin.

If the American South has progressed in the past two hundred years, it is thanks to public and personal repentance—admittedly much of it overseen by the National

Guard, but also thanks to utterly unnatural forgiveness on
the part of the wronged.

Where I live now: in mercy. Repentance. Forgiveness.

Which brings us to my having dinner with Desmond.
Tutu, that is.

The truth of the dinner is that, while my husband and I
were only one table over, a couple of hundred others were
having dinner with Desmond at the same time.

Still, it was a thrill, munching asparagus tips in the same
banquet hall.

After the dinner, he spoke about his work with the
Truth and Reconciliation Commission, and South Africa's
journey from the brutal rule of apartheid to being
led by democratically elected Nelson Mandela, who'd
been imprisoned by the former regime for nearly three
decades.

If ever forgiveness was undeserved and unlikely, surely it
was here. Archbishop Tutu told of atrocities uncovered by
the commission: political opponents of apartheid murdered,
bodies set on fire. And because it takes so long for a human
body to burn to ash, the assassins held their own barbeque
just a few feet away, and popped open some brewskis to
wash it all down. With the crackle and stench of a human
body on fire behind them.

Father, forgive them, Jesus says, *for they do not know what
they are doing.*

Hard, hard words to hear.

During our final year of seminary, two women and I shared a small house in Louisville, Kentucky. Dina and Tracey were smart, compassionate, social activist types. That spring, six years and an eternity before democratic elections in South Africa, Mandela's release was still only a dream and a prayer for those who could bear to pray the impossible. Tracy and Dina and I walked up one evening to the old Vogue Theater to see a movie, *Cry Freedom*, about South Africa. At the film's end, the screen scrolled a long list of activists picked up by the apartheid regime, and related what happened to them in prison: . . . *accidentally fell down seven flights of stairs, and died . . . accidentally fell out four-story window, and died. . . .*

On and on and on the "accidents" scrolled, leaving us weeping and elbowing roommates away from the one available Kleenex.

On the way out of the theater, we ran into a former professor who'd lived in South Africa until the past several years. A white man, he'd worked closely with the anti-apartheid freedom movement. His face had gone from its usual pleasant-but-pasty to utterly ghastly, his whole self colorless.

"What did you think of the film?" one of us asked him—more for something to say than anything.

He held out his right hand. Even in the theater's dim light, we could see that his thumb was raw and bleeding. "I *knew* those people," he said, his voice coming out thick, "those names at the end. I worked with them." His eyes were glazed and confused as he followed our stares at his hand. "I seemed to have pulled the nail off my thumb."

And yet, six years later, the unthinkable happened in South Africa.

Rather than retributive or punitive justice, Desmond Tutu led the country to strive simply for truth, and for forgiveness, for reconciliation and a way forward into the future. Rather than the bloodbath the entire international community predicted, South Africa found its way to magnanimity on the part of the maimed and the suffering.

South Africa, the archbishop suggested, would have been the *last* place in the world anyone would have looked for a model of forgiveness and healing.

Archbishop Tutu paused in his speech, making sure we were paying attention, then whispered this: " 'Precisely,' God says."

It's to the unlikely, the ragged repentant, that Jesus shows up—and revels. It's to those formerly powerless who have every reason to seek and to relish revenge that God gives the greatest of power: to forgive. And find a way forward.

Forgiveness and mercy help patrol my own heart for being ever irked or blasé with what Scott Cairns calls

> . . . *the annoyance*
> *of grace, and this tired music*
> *of salvation.* . . .

It helps to keep posted on the marquis in my mind how deeply in debt I am to forgiveness.

Kyrie eleison, Christe eleison, Kyrie eleison.

And it helps sometimes to hear Jesus speak to the thief on the cross with the criminal record as long as your arm. Jesus also speaking to me. And if I'm listening well, sometimes it sounds something like this—with a Caribbean beat and a South African accent:

You are *soooo* coming with me. Right now. Today.

Welcome to mercy.

10 Hope

The asphalt on which Paul landed had undone his face, his moustache unhooked from his upper lip, his lower jaw unhinged from his upper, his nose relocated far to one side, his eyes swollen shut so that they appeared not to exist except for the mounds of purple where they'd once been. Thrown from the bike he was riding home from a neighborhood development meeting, Paul was the victim of two cars drag racing down a Boston city street.

Paul's own recounting of his accident and recovery focused far more on anguish than physical pain. The time after the accident was a dark night of the soul that lasted many weeks and months of nights.

One of the Massachusetts General janitorial staff members regularly stopped by to sweep or mop. And since she'd heard Paul was a person of faith, she included with every visit an emphatic reminder: "Jesus is here." Paul, in the throes of a harrowing time, was in no mood for anyone offering fluff-fuzzy warmth.

For days and weeks in the hospital, Paul's injuries kept him from speaking, so he scrawled furiously to any of us visiting.

To this woman and her insistent, bulldog's grip on the *Jesus is here*—right there among all the gurgling, dripping feeding and breathing machines—Paul scribbled out, "NO. He is *not*."

"Yep," she said back—said it out loud because she could not write, had never learned how, and because she *could* speak, and, in fact, could get right in his face, "Yep, he is." Being the one standing, she always had the advantage of height, and of strength.

But day after day and dark night after dark night, Paul scribbled away, "NO! He is NOT."

"Yeah," she hammered back, "He is."

And so it went.

There's an old joke about second marriages: the triumph of hope over experience, sustained by the belief that you might not endure the same hurts, miss the same chances, fail again to say what so needed saying. . . .

Hope, we say. *I hope we'll get back to New England this summer*, I e-mail my friend Anne in Massachusetts. Which means I'm penciling in dates, pulling out an old scrapbook of our life in Boston so the kids can remember. But it's hope based on what's going on with my work schedule and my husband's, on finances, on whether beloved friends on the South Shore insist on our staying with them. In average day-speak, hope is intentionally flimsy: nothing I'm staking my life on, or asking anyone else to.

But hope of the sort Jesus teaches and lives springs out of action, not just passive, leather-recliner belief. When the disciples of John the Baptist, who's in prison, approach Jesus, they want to know if he's the one they've hoped would come, the Messiah. Jesus answers with verbs:

> *Go back and report to John what you hear and see:*
> *The blind receive their sight,*
> *the lame walk,*
> *those who have leprosy are cleansed,*
> *the deaf hear,*
> *the dead are raised,*
> *and the good news is proclaimed to the poor.*

In other words, tell John that hope is alive and on the move.

The writers of the Gospels and epistles describe this same high-energy hope: *New birth into a living hope through the resurrection of Jesus Christ from the dead, and into an inheritance that can never perish, spoil, or fade. . . . Set your hope on the grace. . . . Now grace is being sure of what we hope for. . . .* This is more than a little assertive: There is something *out there*, bold and determined. Like the Massachusetts General staff member who clung fast to hope, and spoke of it as she mopped floors of the intensive care unit: *Jesus is here.*

Hope, as it's held up in the form of a cross, has a frightening side. Hope carries with it a well-lit awareness that there will be dark nights of the soul in this life—that there will be accidents and illnesses and betrayals and loneliness. In certain seasons, hope will walk hand in hand with despair. We know all about the reasons that hope is naïve in this case: improbable, impossible. And we cling to a hope that gains strength from the odds stacked against us. This hope finds its source beyond the bleakness of now or the pain of a damaging past.

The way of the Cross begins with suffering, does not try to prettify despair and sorrow and grief, but ends ever in hope. Immanuel, God with us.

Last week, my family and I helped serve dinner at a local shelter. All the families currently living there were single mothers with children. One of them was leaving to move into her own rental house. She was ecstatic, but her eyes flickered with understandable fear, given that life so far had not been full of promises kept. She squared her shoulders. But there was a light behind the bloodshot whites of her eyes. A hope kindled not by experience but by a vision for an ephemeral Could Be out there.

As we drove home, my seven-year-old son Justin observed, "There were only mommies and children there. Where were the daddies?"

Apparently, he expected to hear that they were out grocery shopping, or fixing the canvas tarp over the tree house, or rushing the baby with croup to the doctor.

Under a blonde sheepdog's fringe of bangs, his big eyes blinked, waiting.

My husband and I explained how some daddies did not stay around to grocery shop or walk a cranky infant up and down a hallway all through the night. There were daddies—and mommies—in this world, we explained, who weren't ever present for the children they'd, yes, helped bring into the world.

"But," Justin persisted, "they come back, right? These daddies come back. *Right?*"

It was a statement more than a question.

We circled, then finally landed on what had to be said— that some did not.

"Ever?"

Well . . . for some, not ever, we said.

Justin's face showed he was taking this in, letting it register in the place in his brain where daddies had been catalogued as people who might hold a skillet or catcher's mitt, might put down a newspaper to pick up a book to read to a child. They were *there*. That was how you knew they were daddies.

"Oh, I know," Justin said suddenly, looking relieved. "I get it. It must be that the daddies just *don't know* the mommies need help. If we could just let the daddies know the mommies need help, they'd come back. Right?"

The question hung there in space—held up, perhaps, by naiveté.

Yet, there's something in my son's question I want to cling to, even with my own more cynical view of a world where sometimes people walk out on a child, on a spouse or a lover,

on someone who has every right to expect them to help pull
the red wagon of daily cares. There's an innocent, even holy
insistence in that *Right?* that demands the world be different.
It's a fist in the face of statistics.

Each of the eight years I lived in New England, I swore
to whoever would listen that there had never been so lovely
a spring. The trees that lined the Massachusetts Turnpike
turned pink at their tips, and from there the whole world
burst its seams. A confetti of petals began to fall and color
spilled like overturned paint in puddles of shrubs and
flowering trees and trickles of vines. I sometimes wondered
if those springs were truly more grand, or if they only
seemed so because they followed winters longer and more
brutal than any I'd known growing up in the South. To this
day, I couldn't tell you which.

Like the hope that follows utter darkness, barrenness,
abject despair.

Hope that after a cyclist's being mangled by drag-racing
cars, a human face could be pieced back together—and
that a human soul could find its footing again in faith.

Hope the daddies will understand how much the
mommies need their help, and will come home.

Hope that impossibility would take it in the face this
time, and go down for the count.

Hope that you and that I and they could become
something more courageous, more compassionate, more
reliable and loving and transparently honest than we have
been in the past.

Hope that Jesus has not given us up for worthless—for hopeless.

Years ago, several college friends and I volunteered Thursday evenings at Greenville Group Home, a low-security facility for male juvenile offenders. One of us hatched the clever idea of taking our "boys," most only a couple of years younger than we were, up into the mountains for a day of hiking and the kind of rehab that only the Blue Ridge Mountains can provide. Two of our volunteer group, Stan and Jon, had worked for a boys' camp there, and assured us that the directors would value our working to clear one of the mountain summits for a corral for horses who might travel with certain able equestrian campers on overnight backpacking trips.

We volunteer leaders had our strengths. Jon was an amateur magician, tall and nimble-fingered. Stan could play his guitar and harmonica while driving—playing mostly at stoplights—and he could make his shoulder blades dance like they'd sprung loose from the rest of his back. Janet was an excellent student. But while we were a talented bunch, jaw-dropping hulk didn't figure among our most obvious leadership gifts.

It was only after we'd climbed the mountain, and only after we'd staked out the size of our corral, and only after we'd handed out the axes and knives and machetes that Stan leaned in and quietly observed that perhaps it might have occurred to one of us that young men very like us in size and weight—larger, in fact, than the smaller of us—

young men who'd been convicted of crimes, not terribly pretty, young men of mercurial tempers, perhaps might not be trusted so freely with lethal weapons.

That this was the first it occurred to any of us is less a testimony to our trust in the goodness of humanity than of our not being terribly street-wise. Clearly, a fine liberal arts education increases good common sense not at all.

We realized too late that we'd handed out tools that could be wielded as weapons.

All the horror flicks I'd never seen but knew all about, *Friday the 13th* and *Nightmare on Elm Street,* began flickering in the home theater inside my head: Freddy Krueger leering at me from behind the blackberry scrub we were chopping.

As I recall, we were not attacked that day or sawn into little pieces and left strewn in bite-sized chunks in the woods for forest rangers and foxes to find. Perhaps someone lost his temper, or gave signs it was slipping, but all axes remained aimed at saplings and vines.

One of these boys and I had once had a long conversation in which he insisted that he should commit suicide. He gave a quick sketch of his life, which his case workers later confirmed. He'd witnessed one of his parents murder the other. He'd dropped out of learning, if not of showing up at school, years ago. His skills were hardly that of a third grader. He'd become addicted to various illegal drugs, and still battled cravings. He possessed a long police record for serious theft and drug possession.

"Why," he asked me, "*shouldn't* I kill myself? You tell me why."

I don't recall what I said. Just what I first thought: *Well, good point. I have no idea.*

Because for him things looked utterly hopeless.

Now, we college students were not terribly bright in our little mountain adventure with machetes and mercurial tempers. But like Justin's insistence on things being different some day, I want to hold fast to a hope that believes *all of us*—you and me and young men with criminal records and deadbeat daddies and mommies—yet can live into the *imago Dei*, the image of God.

The hope of the Cross refuses to collapse under the weight of cynicism, bitterness, dismissiveness . . . despair.

The poet Wendell Barry describes a walk through the woods. Here, he found himself standing beside a ragged, half-dead, wild plum tree, old and broken, yet blooming, and he noted, "The great impertinence of beauty / That comes even to the dying."

Surely there's a wild impertinence to our hope.

Impertinent to think that because you prayed for it, despite it's never having turned out in the past, that it might one day be so. You in your insignificant smallness, your trivial interests, your forgettable face, your failure to distinguish yourself, your scandal, your complete lack of integrity. Impertinent to think things would turn out differently this time. Impertinent to think God cared one whit about you.

But sometimes the despair that journeys along with us does us invaluable service—us and our hope.

Because despair leads us to call our old lives what they were: a waste. An exercise in futility. A worshiping of gilded trinkets.

Despair gives us the wisdom to turn our backs on the very mistakes that brought us to the brink. Despair gives us the courage to grasp upward toward hope.

In fact, it's the end that demands new beginning.

Without the stop sign thrust in our paths, we might have rolled on this way indefinitely, deluding ourselves that we were moving forward, onward and upward. When in fact we'd already tanked. Already stalled. Believing ourselves to be living, toward a purpose we never could quite define.

But then comes hope.

"I have found that 'hope,'" the writer Bret Lott told me,

isn't an internal act. It's not about thinking and wishing and, well, *hoping* for something, whether it be a physical need or a spiritual certainty. Hope, at least as far as I have come to understand it, is actually a very physical and proactive and forceful thing to do, and manifests itself in a tremendously physically manner. . . . Hope is lived out. As an author, I hope the book I am writing will work, that it will speak on its own, that God will be glorified through it and that I will be worthy to write it. But this hope must be made manifest by my sitting alone on my butt every day and eking out the next few words that will create the next sentence and next paragraph and chapter and, finally, the next book. Hope won't generate a single word and so will never find its certainty, its answer, without my physical input—without my being there to write *in faith* that next word, and the next. . . . The answer to our hope will always and only be borne out of our physically moving forward in time and space to find that answer.

Deep in the back streets of my city, where metal bars stripe the windows and cars cling close to the corners, a group of women are moving forward in hope.

Last night, I met with a group that included, and honored, women who'd once been prostitutes. Members of Magdalene House. They live in community where they learn to love themselves for the first time, to respect and care for their bodies, to accept that they are tenderly loved by a God who has wept with them there on the corners of Dickerson Pike.

Immanuel. God with us.

One by one, these women came to the mike to read, their words rich and quivering with anguish about lifetimes of abuse and addiction. And now, of hope.

Theirs was no sweet, tentative hope, but a determined, confident hope, an Iwo Jima effort, these women planting a flag in defiance of all their pasts. They touched hands as they walked to the mike, reaching to give the hug of celebration or the nudge forward, their hugs and hands becoming the arms that held the flag together to stake out this place for themselves: this place of safety and freedom. This belief in their own goodness in spite of the years of the needles, the pills, the johns, the men who pulled up to their curbs. Their beauty, their strength. These women who'd been bought and sold for ten dollars, whose worth can't be measured, because God had chosen to claim them. Together, they clung to God and God held them close under a wing where they could rest, and recover, and heal. Their very image, the reflection of God's.

Without exception, the women spoke of sexual abuse as children, and later of drug addiction, then of selling their bodies for money to buy the drugs that masked the pain.

Then a man rose with a guitar in his hand, ambled mikeward, and sang. The lyrics spoke first of seeing a woman on a billboard, then a woman walking down a city street and ogled by men. To these victims of abandonment and abuse, he sang:

> *. . . Every woman used to be*
> *Somebody's little girl.*

This was Nashville, so I didn't need to glance at the program to guess that the bearded singer in faded jeans was the fellow who'd written that song, "I Think About You," Don Schlitz.

Hope found a voice in the lyrics, in the fingers on strings. Hope, finding an echo in our own ill-used, out-of-tune hearts.

We listened, all of us mommies and daddies and sisters and brothers, all of us hookers and swindlers and deceivers and violent and weak, thinking of the little girls in our own homes or circles of friends that we loved, girls growing up into women, and of the women here all around us who'd never gotten to be little girls.

One Magdalene woman, Katrina, poised and elegant, spoke of having been underwater for so long "the water feels safe and comfortable, / But I can't breathe under the water so I have to come up for air." Which is, I believe, the very definition of hope. Of finally realizing, for any of us, you aren't breathing, that in fact you have been drowning for some time now. Whether or not you'd despaired, you should have, had you been paying attention. Yet despair is not the final word. Not the weight that's holding you under, not breathing. There exists a place, as Katrina described it, to surface above the water, to crawl out onto the sand, to see the waves and children laughing and taste the salt of the water and feel the wind and the sun.

The founder of Magdalene House, Becca Stevens, leaned into the mike. "Give a woman a fish and she'll eat for a day. But carve that fish into sushi and serve it up on a platter and give her a glimmer of hope, and that hope will feed her for a lifetime."

Yes. Hope. The battered and stabbed. Hope. Hope hung up on a cross. Hope dead, but not staying dead. . . .

Just over twenty years ago when I showed up in Louisville, Kentucky, to attend theological seminary. I'd neglected to plan ahead for such small details as housing and employment. The folk singer Darrell Adams, his wife Alice, and their two children let me, a stranger—only a friend of a friend, live with them for a time until I could find an apartment. When I left their house, they sent me off with gifts—both big hugs and also my first pieces of furniture: a bed, where I slept throughout my single adult years and where my children have slept, and a Bentwood rocker that's somehow survived my past ninety-five moves.

My favorite song that Darrell performs, old Ira P. Stamphill lyrics, admits the often appalling uncertainty and fragility of life. The chorus insists,

Many things about tomorrow I don't seem to understand
But I know who holds tomorrow and I know who holds my hand.

I can hear Darrell's rich, mellow voice and his acoustic guitar. And see Alice smiling at me from the kitchen.

Just last weekend, the old wooden bed they gave me two decades ago as I began a hopeful new season of life was passed on to a family just leaving a homeless shelter for a hopeful new season of their own. Hope: sometimes passed on in word, and sometimes in the form of slats and a sturdy headboard.

Here's what little I know about Darrell and Alice:

They took me in, and probably others, when I was a stranger.

They followed a calling, this music, when there were no financial guarantees.

They've since lost one of their two gorgeous children— their son—to a tragic car wreck.

"Tomorrow" did not turn out according to plan.

They are held. Somewhere beneath the cyclone of sorrow are the everlasting arms.

They are passionately, unflaggingly loved by the One who journeys beside them, Immanuel. Or in the words of the Massachusetts General janitorial staff member, hard as they may be to trust: *Jesus is here.*

This hope we claim means there will someday be a grand family reunion the likes of which we've never seen. There will be music, I'm certain—folk music first, bluegrass and country and blues, and then, who knows, rap, where the lyrics are wildly, outrageously hopeful. The place will be thick in streamers and golden balloons, and families and friends parted by that spoiler death will be throwing themselves into full-bodied, flying-leap hugs.

Karl Marx famously labeled faith "the opiate of the people," promising an afterlife in which things will be better.

Maybe.

Or maybe it's more like a spine.

Maybe it's hope that draws its very strength from having stood toe to toe with despair, and come out on top.

Because Jesus promises not only a Tomorrow of celebration, the party to end all parties, but also hope in the storm-ravaged Now.

Hope that will not forsake us.

Not in the Valley of the Shadow of Death.

Not in a life shipwrecked by drugs and abuse.

Not in the face of a criminal record and a past mangled by pain.

Hope . . . lived out, passed hand to hand and voice to voice.

Hope, the only answer to death.

Hope, the only lifeline to tomorrow.

Hope, the impertinent. The beautiful-bold.

Hope, the fist in the face of despair.

Acknowledgments

My warmest, deepest, widest thanks—

To Lil Copan, first for being interested in seeing this book in its earliest, ugliest form and later for helping bring order from chaos. And to the rest of the fine people of Paraclete Press for their insights, support, and hard work.

To all those who have allowed me to tell stories involving them, or share thoughts quoting them, or been generous with their time in helping me think about what these particular words of faith might mean if taken seriously: Alice Adams, Darrell Adams, Sara Bahner, Jeff Barneson, Paul Bothwell, Ginger Brasher-Cunningham, Milton Brasher-Cunningham, Kay Price Brinkley, Jon Brooks, Pete Cernoia, Jay R. Clover, Kitty Freeman Gay, Amy Jo Girardier, Beth Harris, Scott Harris, Beth Jackson-Jordan, Dasha Johnson, David Jordan, Diane Jordan, Monty Jordan, Lisa Lamb, Rich Lamb, Susan Bahner Lancaster, Bret Lott, Kyle Matthews, Susan Matthews, Christine Kim Mihevc, Anne Moore, Julie Pennington-Russell, Stephanie Powers, Rick Sams, Teri Sams, Kelly Shushok, Laura Singleton, Becca Stevens, Chris Treadwell, Chuck Treadwell, Carol Vicary, John Vicary and the BBC Vicary class, Mike Willard, Stan Wilson, Bob Yinger, and Janet Yinger.

To Tony Campolo, Lauren Winner, Scot McKnight, and Kelly Monroe Kullberg, writers and speakers who took time they did not have to read this book.

To the world's greatest daughters and son, Jasmine, Julia, and Justin Jordan-Lake, who never get to give their official permission for the stories their mother tells about them, but who suffer this indignity ever graciously.

And to Todd, magnificent in his patience, wisdom, wit, insight, and support. I cannot imagine a finer, funnier, or more fascinating life companion.

Living into Those Alarming Words

Questions for Discussion or Contemplation

1 Resurrection

Scripture readings of the four gospel resurrection accounts:
Matthew 28:1–20; Mark 16:1–8; Luke 24:1–53; John 20:1–31

1. What associations—both positive and negative—do you have with the words *resurrection* or *risen*?

2. Thinking about your own past, what is appealing about a death of the old life and starting over? Is anything about that idea disturbing?

3. The author refers to "David the Royal Screw Up." What other biblical characters, early church leaders, saints, or generally respected cultural figures who also fit this general characterization come to your mind? Read Psalm 52 aloud. What particular phrases stand out to you?

4. The seventeenth-century poet John Donne envisions a new life of faith beginning with a violent overthrow of

the old. Does this idea of violence add anything to your thinking about a real-life experience of resurrection?

5. Describe one person (perhaps yourself) whose present situation appears to be absolutely beyond redemption. What would it take, do you think, for that person to live into resurrection? If you are in a group discussion, feel free to change or omit actual names.

6. Picturing your own inner life or that of someone close to you, if someone were to snap *Extreme Makeover Home Edition* "before" and "after" shots—or just "before"— what would they look like? Try avoiding church or spiritual language and instead use construction terminology; for example, foundation, rot, structural integrity, renovation, razing, etc.

2 Community

1. Write or tell a brief story describing a time in your life in which a particular community—whether family, neighbors, professional colleagues, or a community of faith—helped share your grief, stress, or concerns.

2. Describe a time in your life when you helped shoulder the load of someone else's grief or concerns.

3. In what ways have you seen communities of faith do an extraordinarily good or horrifically poor job of sharing one another's celebrations and sorrows?

4. Ideally, how *should* people of faith be a transformative kind of community? Give specific examples of what you've observed, or what you wish you'd seen instead.

5. If you've ever participated in the sacrament of communion, describe a time when you were particularly struck with the people around you and your connection to them through that service.

6. By nature, do you lean more toward interconnectedness or an attitude of I Can Do It by Myself? How does this impact your spiritual journey?

3 Abundance

1. In what situations do you most often experience greed? How do you handle these situations, both in the moment and later in reflecting on them?

2. In what ways might the pursuit of material abundance drive any part of your life, such as your educational or professional goals?

3. Read the parable of the rich man with his bigger and better barns in Luke 12:16–21. If you were to set this story in a contemporary context, what would replace the barns?

4. If you were to point to one area of material excess in your life, what would that be?

5. Describe a time when you longed for a certain material item and finally acquired it. What happened next?

6. The author quotes T.S. Eliot's describing his culture as a "decent godless people / Their only monument the asphalt road / And a thousand lost golf balls." What specific images would you use to symbolize the culture you live in?

7. In what ways does the word *abundance* describe or not describe your life?

8. What are some specific steps you could take to help you focus on God's abundance?

4 Wisdom

1. What is your personal definition of wisdom?

2. Describe a time when you have tried to appear to be something or someone you were not.

3. Looking at those lives close to you and your own life, do you see any truth to the old saying "older but wiser"?

4. When have you witnessed remarkable wisdom particularly of a spiritual sort—in a young person?

5 Holiness

1. Does the word *holiness* have positive connotations for you? Along these lines, if holiness were a person, what would he or she look like?

2. With the idea of Jesus as merely the dispenser of cheap, easy grace, how would you rewrite the Ten Commandments in modern-day language?

3. Can shame ever serve a useful purpose in a spiritual journey?

4. In terms of Christian practices such as fasting, silence, reading Scripture, or a daily rhythm of prayer, what if anything have you found helpful in the past in your own pursuit of holiness? If your spiritual journey is in its early stages, what practices do you find most daunting?

5. What are some specific ways in which you could reorder your days to chisel out time for spiritual disciplines?

6. What role does solitude play in your life? Is solitude something you crave more of, or something that makes you uneasy after a short time? How important should it be in a spiritual journey?

7. Try making a list of the optional uses of your time—not, for example, showering or feeding the dog. Are there days in which TV could be omitted or lunch skipped?

6 Peace

1. In many traditional church settings, discussions of *peace* focus exclusively on personal feelings of contentment or lack of disruption. What is the range of Jesus' distinct references to peace?

2. If Jesus is the "Prince of Peace," as Isaiah prophesies, how does this guide your understanding of a spiritual journey?

3. Do faith communities have a responsibility to be involved in—or at least knowledgeable about—politics and issues of world peace? If not, why not? If so, in what ways?

4. Describe a time in which you encountered someone you instinctively and actively disliked. Were you ashamed of your feelings or do you believe they were justified?

5. Would you classify yourself as being of the "flight" or "fight" species? How does this impact your ability or give you difficulty in handling conflict?

6. Do you think of yourself as having enemies? Without using an actual name, describe why they've earned your hostility, or you've earned theirs. In active, real-life terms, what does it mean to love one's enemies? What would it take in your life to accomplish this?

7. Think outside the box. What specific activitiy or involvement might you be willing to try in order to stretch your own understanding of living into peace?

8. In what ways do followers of Christ do an exemplary job of promoting peace, however you choose to define that word? In what ways not?

9. On the national or international scene, what do you consider to be the most hopeless situation in terms of the lack of peace? What does it mean to pray for peace? Is it naïve? Is it helpful? What specific practices might accompany praying for peace?

10. How are personal peace and world peace related, or are they?

7 Blessedness

Scripture references: Matthew 5:1–12 and Luke 6:17–26.

1. Be brutally honest: In what ways do you tend to categorize people? What about the family or culture in which you were raised prepared you to do this?

2. Are there healthy ways of dividing people?

3. Why would the nativity story of Jesus feature characters of little education and low socioeconomic standing? If you were to write yourself into the story, where would you show up?

4. Describe a time when someone else made assumptions about you that were wrong, and perhaps offensive. What about a time when you made assumptions about someone else?

5. Read the Beatitudes in the gospel accounts of Matthew and Luke (see Scripture references above). Try putting these in contemporary language that makes sense in your own cultural context.

6. Is there anything about these "Blessed are . . . " statements of Jesus' that you find just a little unfair or alarming?

7. If you had to choose one of the "Blessed are" statements in Matthew or Luke to hang your name beside, which fits you most closely in this season of your life?

8 Worship

1. What is your definition of worship?

2. What factors contribute to your being able to worship well? What impedes your ability to worship?

3. Should worship be linked with ideas of serving the poor? Is this in any way in conflict with traditional ideas of worship?

4. What are some instances of worship found in Scripture?

5. Not limiting your answer to worship that takes place in a church sanctuary, describe a time of profound worship for you. What factors in your own life or in the setting contributed to this?

6. Specifically, what changes in your own life would you need to make in order to transform your ability to worship?

7. Does any aspect of offering up all that we are and all that we have to God make you uncomfortable? If so, why, and how might that change?

9 Forgiveness

1. Describe a time when you received some form of mercy or forgiveness you absolutely did not deserve.

2. Name a time when you really longed for revenge. Did you get it? If so, how did it feel?

3. What grudge are you presently holding? What would it take for you to let go of that?

4. Is there anyone in your life you feel justified in despising? Do you spend much time thinking about this person? What impact does that have on you?

5. Think of a specific time when you really screwed up and hurt someone else. Did that other person eventually offer forgiveness? If so, describe that. If not, where does that leave you, and where do you go from here?

6. Think of a time when you knew you'd royally blown it. Have you felt entirely forgiven by God, regardless of any other people involved? How has that impacted your relationship with or thinking about God?

7. If you had been a South African victim of apartheid, how would you have reacted to pleas for truth and reconciliation?

8. Specifically, what concrete steps might you take to implement forgiveness in an area of your own life where it has been lacking?

10 Hope

1. Describe a time in your life in which you felt utterly hopeless, or when you were completely convinced of God's absence.

2. Picture someone close to you—or perhaps yourself—in a seemingly hopeless situation. Does clinging to hope in this case seem naïve, unreasonable, or patently insane?

3. Why might hope be described as impertinent?

4. If hope were a person, how might he or she look?

5. Do any aspects of hope make you uncomfortable? If so, why?

6. What are some material or tangible ways in which you could pass on hope to someone else, just as the old wooden bed was passed on?

7. What would it look like in your own life if you were to live out this idea of hope more actively and concretely? Try making a list of what you envision.

Notes

1 Resurrection

Resurrection accounts of Jesus appear in each of the four New Testament Gospels: Matthew 28:1–20; Mark 16:1–8; Luke 24:1–53; John 20:1–31.

p. 2   *"Less monstrous, / for our own convenience, our own sense of beauty."*
John Updike, "Seven Stanzas at Easter" first published in *The Christian Century*, Feb. 22, 1961, p. 236; later included in *Telephone Poles and Other Poems* (New York: A. Knopf, 1961).

p. 7   *"Batter my heart, three-person'd God; for You / As yet but knock, breathe, shine. . . ."*
John Donne, "Batter My Heart," *Holy Sonnets, The Selected Poetry of Donne* (New York: New American Library, 1966), p. 271.

p. 11   *"Death, thou shalt die."*
John Donne, "Death Be Not Proud," *Holy Sonnets, The Selected Poetry of Donne* (New York: New American Library, 1966), p. 270.

3 Abundance

p. 25   *When he's approached by the earnest young Fortune 500 CEO. . . .*
Luke 18:18–24.

p. 26   *The Great Gatsby.*
A novel by F. Scott Fitzgerald.

p. 27   *The story Jesus tells of the man who builds a bigger barn. . . .*
Luke 12:16–21.

p. 29   *T.S. Eliot described as a "decent godless people."*
T.S. Eliot, "Choruses from the Rock," *The Complete Poems and Play, 1909–50* (New York: Harcourt Brace Jovanovich, 1952), p. 103.

p. 29   *Miroslav Volf: that what we give to God's right hand is only what we've taken from God's left.*
An idea explored in his book *Free of Charge.*

4 Wisdom

p. 32   *. . . You do not belong to the world. . . .*
John 15:19.

p. 35   *'What franticke fit,' quoth he, 'hath thus distraught / Thee, foolish man. . . .'*
Edmund Spenser, *The Faerie Queene,* I. ix. 38 (New York: Norton, 1968), p. 106.

p. 36   John 3:16.
For God so loved the world that he gave his only Son that whoever believes in him shall not perish but have eternal life.

p. 36   *Come thou fount of every blessing, / Tune my heart to sing thy praise. . . .*
The lyrics of "Come Thou Fount of Every Blessing" were written by Robert Robinson (1735–90).

p. 37   *All . . . have sinned and fall short of the glory of God.*
Romans 3:23.

p. 39   *O, to grace how great a debtor. . . .*
From "Come Thou Fount of Every Blessing" (see above).

p. 41   *"Take it and read."*
Saint Augustine, *Confessions,* Book viii.12 (New York: Penguin, 1961), p. 177.

p. 41   *All three synoptic Gospels recount Jesus' rebuke to his followers and embrace of the kids.*
Matthew 19:13–15; Mark 10:13–16; Luke 18:15–17.

p. 41   Emerson Hall houses the philosophy department of Harvard.

p. 42   *"What Is Man That Thou Are Mindful of Him . . . ?"*
Psalm 8:4 (KJV).

5 Holiness

p. 44   *"Holiness," said Walter Rauschenbusch, "is goodness on fire."*
Quoted in Richard Foster, *Streams of Living Water: Celebrating the Traditions of Christian Faith* (HarperSanFrancisco, 1998), p. 59.

p. 45   *"Binding with briars [our] joys and desires," as William Blake wrote.*
William Blake, "The Garden of Love," *Selected Poems* (New York: Oxford University Press, 1996), p. 123.

p. 45   *You've heard it was said . . . but I tell you. . . .*
Scriptural references include Matthew 5:21–22, 27–28, 31–32, 38–39, 43–44; 12:6; 17:12; 26:29; Mark 9:13; Luke 4:25; 6:27; 9:27.

p. 51   *With Jesus, holiness is never about our woundedness but his.*
Henri Nouwen's book *The Wounded Healer* explores this idea.

p. 51   *Cling to what is good, be devoted . . . keep your spiritual fervor serving. . . ."*
A loose translation of Romans 12:9–11.

p. 52   *Years ago, I'd met the corporation's founder. . . .*
Truett Cathy is the founder of Chick-Fil-A Corporation.

p. 53   *And the saints are just the sinners / Who fall down, and get up.*
From the song "We Fall Down," music and lyrics by Kyle Matthews. Copyright © 1997 BMG Songs, Inc. Used with permission. BMG, Inc., License #: 275740. All rights reserved.

p. 55   *Sometimes a path toward holiness—and with holiness. . . .*
Some excellent books on spiritual disciplines and spiritual formation include Eugene Peterson's *A Long Obedience in the Same Direction;* Lauren Winner's *Mudhouse Sabbath;* Dallas Willard's *Renovation of the Heart;* Dorothy Bass's *Receiving the Day;* Richard Foster's *Prayer* and *Celebration of Discipline;* and many books by Henri Nouwen.

p. 61   *The late short story writer Andre Dubus.*
The late Andre Dubus's *Meditations from a Moveable Chair,* as well as his collections of short stories.

6 Peace

p. 64   *You have heard that it was said, "Love your neighbors and hate your enemy. . . ."*
cf. Matthew 5:43–48.

p. 65   *If your enemy is hungry, feed him / if he is thirsty, give him something to drink. . . .*
Romans 12:20 and Proverbs 25:21–22.

p. 66   *Live in harmony with one another. Do not be proud. . . .*
Romans 12:16–19.

p. 68   *It was the Peace-At-All-Costs . . . Harriet Beecher Stowe's* Uncle Tom's Cabin. . . .
See Joy Jordan-Lake, *Whitewashing* Uncle Tom's Cabin: *Nineteenth-Century Women Novelists Respond to Stowe* (Nashville: Vanderbilt University Press, 2005).

p. 70   *Just War Theory.*
         Briefly stated, Saint Augustine's Just War Theory involves
         prerequisites that must be met for a war to qualify as
         "just":
         • the war can only be justified by the clear and damaging
           injustice of an aggressor;
         • right intentions: in other words a hope of establishing
           or restoring peace, never revenge or retaliation;
         • violence must never pass a point exceeding the original
           injustice;
         • last resort: all other avenues of diplomacy and other
           pressures must have been exhausted;
         • discrimination between civilians and combatants: the
           war must be waged in such a way as to protect the
           safety of innocent noncombatants.

p. 70   *Father, forgive them. . . .*
         Luke 23:34.

p. 71   *Catherine of Siena refers to God as "pierced wine-barrel," with
         love overflowing and intoxicating our every impulse.*
         Catherine of Siena, quoted in *Incandescence,* ed. Carmen
         Acevedo Butcher (Brewster, MA: Paraclete Press, 2005),
         p. 80.

p. 72   *Not "Blessed are the peacelovers," but "Blessed are the
         peacemakers."*
         Matthew 5:9.

p. 72   *Justice falling down in torrents.*
         A loose translation of Amos 5:24.

p. 72   *You [God] fill our understanding with joy and light. . . .*
         Catherine of Siena, *Incandescence,* p. 80.

p. 73   *Children of God, as Jesus called it.*
         A reference to Jesus' saying: "Blessed are the peacemakers,
         for they will be called children of God" (Matthew 5:9).

p. 73   *Glory to God in the highest heaven, and on earth peace.*
Luke 2:14.

p. 74   *Landmines, for example. Small things that kill as many as twenty thousand people a year, 80 percent of those killed, civilians.*
www.unicef.org/media/media_24360.html.

p. 74   *T.S. Eliot quotes Julian of Norwich when he writes, "And all shall be well. . . ."*
T.S. Eliot, "Little Gidding," *The Four Quartets*, *The Complete Poems and Plays, 1909–50* (New York: Harcourt Brace Jovanovich, 1952), p. 144.

p. 75   *I did not come to bring peace to the earth, but a sword.*
Matthew 10:34.

7 Blessedness

p. 85   *Abiding in the field.*
Luke 2:8 (KJV).

p. 85   *In his poem "At the Manger," one of W. H. Auden's shepherds comments that they have "walked a thousand miles yet only worn / The grass between our work and home away."*
W.H. Auden, "At the Manger," *Collected Poems*, ed. Edward Mendelson (New York: Vintage Books, 1991), p. 381.

p. 87   *Blessed are you because true blessings have nothing to do with money, and money can trip you up badly, like that poor rich young ruler, in the path to finding true riches.*
cf. Matthew 19:16–30; Mark 10:17–31; Luke 18:18–30.

8 Worship

p. 90   *A group of us had read the fifty-eighth chapter of the prophet Isaiah. . . .*
Isaiah 58:1–14.

p. 91   *Jesus walks on the water to them. Despite the lack of firm
        footing. . . .*
        cf. Matthew 14:22–33. I'm indebted to John Vicary's
        Bible study for insights into this passage.

p. 91   *New Testament worship   gorgeous acts of absurd faith and
        near felonies. . . .*
        cf. Matthew 9:1–8; Mark 2:1–12; Luke 5:17–26.

p. 91   *Pleading for the healing of her daughter, a desperate Canaanite
        woman. . . .*
        cf. Matthew 15:21–28.

p. 91   *In fact, when Jesus does show up in official houses of worship.*
        . . .
        cf. Matthew 21:12–13; Mark 11:15–19; Luke 19:45–46;
        John 2:13–25.

p. 93   *We told and re-told each other how Jesus multiplied loaves and
        fishes. . . .*
        Accounts of multiplying loaves and fishes, also called
        the Feeding of the Multitudes or the Feeding of the
        Five Thousand and the Feeding of the Four Thousand,
        appear in Matthew 14:13–21; 15:32–39; Mark 6:30–44;
        8:1–10; Luke 9:10–17; and John 6:5–14.

p. 96   *The word worship . . . And the -ship of the worth/worship.*
        Timely e-mails from Sara Bahner and Susan Bahner
        Lancaster were invaluable reminders of the etymology
        of these words. E-mail correspondence, March 2007.

p.101   *. . . to proclaim good news to the poor. . . .*
        Isaiah 61:1–3; cf. Luke 4:16–20.

9 Forgiveness

p. 109 *"A golden ladder on one side, a coal chute on the other."*
        Billy Collins, "The Afterlife," *Questions about Angels:*

Poems. (Pittsburgh: University of Pittsburgh Press, 1999), p. 33.

p. 117   *That depends, Jesus responds. How many times would you like God to forgive you?*
A paraphrase of Luke 6:37 and implied in Matthew 6:14–15, 18:35; Mark 11:25.

p. 118   *Father, forgive them . . . for they do not know what they are doing.*
Luke 23:34.

p. 120   *. . . The annoyance / of grace, and this tired music / of salvation. . . .*
Scott Cairns, "Salvation," *Philokalia* (Lincoln, NB: Zoo Press, 2002), p. 54.

p. 120   *Kyrie eleison, Christe eleison, Kyrie eleison.*
Lord have mercy, Christ have mercy, Lord have mercy.

10 Hope

p. 124   *Go back and report to John what you hear and see: . . .*
Matthew 11:4–5.

p. 124   *New birth into a living hope through the resurrection of Jesus Christ. . . .*
1 Peter 1:3–4, 13; Hebrews 11:1; cf. Romans 5:3–4.

p. 130   *"The great impertinence of beauty / That comes even to the dying."*
Wendell Berry, *A Timbered Choir: The Sabbath Poems 1979–97* (Washington, D.C.: Counterpoint, 1998), p. 87.

p. 131   *"Hope isn't an internal act. It's not about thinking and wishing . . ."*
Novelist Bret Lott was kind enough to respond to an e-mail I sent to several friends and colleagues requesting

their personal insights on theological matters. E-mail correspondence, February 2007.

p. 132   *Members of Magdalene House.*

The women of Magdalene also run the nonprofit business Thistle Farms, which sells personal care products made from ingredients grown and harvested by the women and their supporters.

p. 133   *Every woman used to be / Somebody's little girl.*

Don Schlitz wrote the song "I Think About You."

p. 135   *Many things about tomorrow I don't seem to understand / But I know who holds tomorrow and I know who holds my hand.*

Lyrics of "I Know Who Holds Tomorrow" by Ira P. Stamphill.

ABOUT PARACLETE PRESS

WHO WE ARE

Paraclete Press is an ecumenical publisher of books and recordings on Christian spirituality. Our publishing represents a full expression of Christian belief and practice—from Catholic to Evangelical, from Protestant to Orthodox.

Paraclete Press is the publishing arm of the Community of Jesus, an ecumenical monastic community in the Benedictine tradition. As such, we are uniquely positioned in the marketplace without connection to a large corporation and with informal relationships to many branches and denominations of faith.

We like it best when people buy our books from booksellers, our partners in successfully reaching as wide an audience as possible.

WHAT WE ARE DOING

Books

Paraclete Press publishes books that show the richness and depth of what it means to be Christian. Although Benedictine spirituality is at the heart of all that we do, we publish books that reflect the Christian experience across many cultures, time periods, and houses of worship.

We publish books that nourish the vibrant life of the church and its people—books about spiritual practice, formation, history, ideas, and customs.

We have several different series of books within Paraclete Press, including the best-selling Living Library series of modernized classic texts; A Voice from the Monastery—giving voice to men and women monastics about what it means to live a spiritual life today; award-winning literary faith fiction; and books that explore Judaism and Islam and discover how these faiths inform Christian thought and practice.

Recordings

From Gregorian chant to contemporary American choral works, our music recordings celebrate the richness of sacred choral music through the centuries. Paraclete is proud to distribute the recordings of the internationally acclaimed choir Gloriæ Dei Cantores, who have been praised for their "rapt and fathomless spiritual intensity" by *American Record Guide,* and the Gloriæ Dei Cantores Schola, which specializes in the study and performance of Gregorian chant. Paraclete is also the exclusive North American distributor of the recordings of the Monastic Choir of St. Peter's Abbey in Solesmes, France, long considered to be a leading authority on Gregorian chant performance.

Learn more about us at our Web site:
www.paracletepress.com,
or call us toll-free at 1-800-451-5006.

Also Available . . .

Mudhouse Sabbath

$14.95, trade paper
978-1-55725-532-7

After her conversion from Orthodox Judaism to Christianity, Lauren Winner found that her life was indelibly marked by the rich traditions and spiritual practices of Judaism. She presents eleven Jewish spiritual practices that can transform the way Christians view the world, and God.

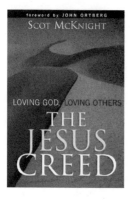

The Jesus Creed

$16.95, trade paper
978-1-55725-400-9

When an expert in the law asked Jesus for the greatest commandment, Jesus responded with the *Shema*, the ancient Jewish creed that commands Israel to love God with heart, soul, mind, and strength. But the next part of Jesus' answer would change the course of history. Jesus amended the *Shema*, giving his followers a new creed for life: to love God with heart, soul, mind, and strength, but also to love others as themselves.

Available from most booksellers or through Paraclete Press: www.paracletepress.com; 1-800-451-5006. Try your local bookstore first.